A volume in the Hyperion reprint series
THE RADICAL TRADITION IN AMERICA

HYPERION PRESS, INC.
Westport, Connecticut

Elder, Henry C. Blinn.

A

CONCISE HISTORY

OF

THE UNITED SOCIETY OF BELIEVERS

CALLED

SHAKERS

BY

CHARLES EDSON ROBINSON

ILLUSTRATED

EAST CANTERBURY
N H

Published in 1893 at Shaker Village, East Canterbury, N.H.
Copyright 1893 by Charles Edson Robinson
Hyperion reprint edition 1975
Library of Congress Catalog Number 75-342
ISBN 0-88355-245-0
Printed in the United States of America

Library of Congress Cataloging in Publication Data

Robinson, Charles Edson, 1836-1925.
  A concise history of the United Society of Believers
called Shakers.

  (The Radical tradition in America)
  Reprint of the ed. printed at East Canterbury, N.H.
  1. Shakers—United States.   I.   Title.
BX9766.R6   1975   289.8'0973   75-342
ISBN 0-88355-245-0

PREFACE.

THIS little work is the outcome of a series of papers on Communism, the publication of which was begun in "The Manufacturer and Builder," a New York monthly, in the January issue of 1891, and is still, at the present time, being continued in that Journal, under the *nom de plume* of C. R. Edson.

The first of the papers in the series treated somewhat briefly of the relation of capital and labor; of the theories advanced by Edward Bellamy in his "Looking Backward;" of the peculiar, "recent inaugural address of Mayor Sargent of New Haven, following with the remark that, "How far these communistic ideas, which are spread so broadcast, are the outcome of an ardent and honest desire on the part of the individual to benefit the poorer classes of the community, or of a desire to be a promoter in the scheme, and thus reap financial or political benefit as a leader, it is not easy to determine." The statement was then made that "The communistic societies have been legion, and they have had as champions in their day some of the most talented minds in America. Five of these associations were inaugurated in the last century, and sixty-eight from 1819 to 1853 inclusive, but that forty-five of them died young, and the most of them in the second year of their existence."

The publication of these papers called out a lively correspondence, which was published in the same journal, between John C. Trautwine, Esq., of Philadelphia, a prominent member of the Franklin Institute of that city, one of the oldest scientific institutions in the country, in which he most vigorously advocated the adoption of a political, governmental form of communism after the plan as set forth in Bellamy's "Looking Backward," and the author of the communistic papers, who, in a series of letters advanced arguments showing the utter impracticability of such a scheme under the natural, selfish tendency of mankind for oppression; that a political, governmental communism could never be made a success until the human family are willing to submit to a higher power for their guidance, and to thoroughly eradicate every feature of selfishness from society as has the doctrine of Shakerism extirpated, root and branch, selfishness from their Community.

The writer makes no claim to originality, except in the arrangement of the matter which has been placed at his disposal. The great aim and end sought for has been to collect facts in relation to the Shakers and state them so clearly that the world may know, as they read, of the true life and habits of this most singular people. Their upright dealing and strict honesty, individually and collectively, all persons can testify to who have ever been brought into business relations with them. No Shaker was ever known to make a false statement in relation to any business transaction whatever.

Much has been written derogatory of the Shakers, but they have outlived all of the calumny heaped without measure, in the past, upon their heads. The world has come to see that vile characters are not to be found in the Shaker ranks, as their Society is one of the last places on earth that persons of a shady reputation would seek in which to ply their trade.

Of the future of Shakerism and the question as to whether they will exist as a body to pass the two hundredth mile-stone of their years, is a matter for speculation. Great and stirring events are crowding fast upon us as a nation. What will be our fate when the year 1976 shall have been reached it is hard for us to foretell. The vast concentration of capital in a few individual hands and the great and growing unrest of the laboring multitude bodes no good in the Community. The rumbling of the volcano of discontent now heard in the distance may break out in our midst without further warning and bring us face to face in a conflict of the same nature as has been the death-knell of other once powerful and prosperous nations of earth of whom we now have only monumental piles of ruin to mark their once flourishing marts.

That Shakerism will endure the ravages of time as long as other Christian denominations exist, we see no reason to doubt. That the Shakers in their daily lives are but following in the footsteps of Jesus and his apostles is too self-evident for refutation.

CHARLES EDSON ROBINSON.

New York, May 15, 1893.

PREFACE BY THE PUBLISHER.

In the goodness of Divine Providence a very acceptable gift has been conferred upon our Community, and whatever may be said of the unseen forces that inspire the heart and move the pen in the interests of humanity and through this medium for the glory of God, we see in this most worthy act of kindness of man toward man, that which places the matter, embodied in this little work so closely to the realm of inspiration, that we are quite pleased to look upon it as coming from the spirit of God, through the spirit of man.

The writer of the following pages although a stranger to nearly all who, at present, reside in the Community at Canterbury, was during the years of his childhood a resident of the beautiful village of East Concord, N. H., about eight miles distant from the Shakers. Through the visitation of some pleasant influences still resting on the mind, he has passed along the journey of life unprejudiced and been permitted to write of the Community of Shakers as he would write of the interests that demand his daily attention.

Unsolicited as the whole subject has been by us, and appearing in the columns of the "Manufacturer and Builder," written in such a gentlemanly and liberal spirit, it has induced the directors of our Community to suggest its publication in book form, as we might, in that way, not only manifest our appreciation of the work, but be able to place before our readers a concise statement of the origin of the Community, as well as its progress in the religious world, and in this way allow the Christian Communistic Order to become more generally known.

Our suggestion was not only very cordially acceded to by our friend, the author, but he at once arranged the entire work suitably for the use of the printers. It was the free-will gift of a liberal mind, and becomes of peculiar worth to us on account of having been written by a person not especially interested in the religious doctrines of the Shakers, nor by the solicitation of any of its members.

That there may be some illustrations of the Shakers and of Shakerism not in perfect accord with the manner in which a Shaker would express them, is not, in the least, a matter of surprise, nor a point in the use of language, over which we need dwell for a moment. The author, Charles E. Robinson, has demonstrated with perspicuity the system of Communism as it has been and is now known among the Shakers. He has shown conclusively that the pages of sacred and profane history bear witness of the same order of life, which has led more or less of the family of man to turn their attention to a deeper consecration of their lives for the good of their brother man.

Even the devoted life of Jesus and no less that of his disciples is a striking exemplification of this noted fact, and through this we are led to believe that any man or woman whose life is consecrated to God can not otherwise than develop a system of Christian Communism, the same as taught by Jesus, the Christ.

The witnesses of God for this religious work were evidently under the same spiritual ministration as that which came upon the primitive Church, and gave to them new tongues, through which to speak in praise to God, and enable them to live a new life of practical righteousness. If the testimony of Shakerism bears any other stamp than the gospel of Christ, then indeed, it is not what it purports to be.

As Jesus formed his little society of such persons as were willing to accept his gospel ministry, he found them just as the life of the world had developed them, in that selfishness so characteristic of the natural man. Mother Ann and the Elders could not do otherwise than meet the people as they stood in their worldly relations. Their harvest fields were in the cities of Babylon, and amidst the confusion of tongues. It was the forming of the untried elements of the world into a Community of religious interests. All the habits and practices of an unregenerate class were brought to the front and made doubly conspicuous by their presence in a select body. Accepting as some did, a religious zeal without sufficient weight to guide it, they broke forth into a religious wild fire and returned to the world, in language and manners, just what they had taken from it. The same result would evidently occur to-day under corresponding circumstances.

From that time to the present date, there has been a gradual increase in the growth of the Community, till a life of practical righteousness, as understood by the light of to-day forms the leading feature. To be "pure and peaceable, gentle, easy to be entreated and without hypocrisy," is of far more consequence in the promotion of peace and happiness in a Community than can be any system of outward observances.

The language, the dress, the food and the general customs of the Society must change, more or less, through the growth of intelligence, through the privilege of association and through the demands of necessity. To meet these judiciously must be by a system of economy, that no harm may arise to the Community in passing from one degree of travel to another.

A thorough investigation of this religious system is solicited, and if it can not bear the crucial test of the professor and the profane, in the light of the present day, then it should be exposed and relegated to the realms of Pluto. That we may be thoroughly understood in the mission which we have accepted, we would invite the investigator to peruse, carefully, the publications of the Community, and see upon what kind of a foundation we have established our hope.

HENRY C. BLINN.

East Canterbury, N. H. May 15, 1893.

CONTENTS.

INTRODUCTION.

ANCIENT COMMUNISM.

viii

CHAPTER XV.

CHAPTER XVI.

CHAPTER XVII.

CHAPTER XVIII.

CHAPTER XIX.

ILLUSTRATIONS.

FAMILY DWELLING, SHAKERS, SABBATHDAY LAKE, ME.

David Parker, Trustee.

INTRODUCTION.

————◆————

ANCIENT COMMUNISM—ESSENES, THE FORERUNNERS OF THE AMERICAN SHAKERS.

COMMUNISM is found to be one of the first organized forms of Society, as old as history itself. In the days of Abraham of old, men dwelt in tents and held their property in common. One thousand years later, we find a system of communism established in Sparta, by that famous lawgiver, Lycurgus, such as the world never saw.

The founders of the Christian Church were communists in every sense of the word. In fact it is the foundation stone found underlying all forms of religion. More than two thousand years before the advent of Christ we learn from the words of the sacred Hindoo bible Ramayana, of the birth of Chrishna, the story of whose life is more fully told in the Baghavat Gita, the episode portion of the Mahabrat bible, which book is believed by the Hindoos as divinely inspired, and to have an antiquity of six thousand years.

Chrishna had hosts of earnest followers, who, like himself, were baptized in the river Ganges. His life, and that of his followers, was one of communism. They held all things in common. He taught the doctrine of equality for all men. From one common fund all expenses were met. His precepts display profound wisdom, and are not to be improved upon by any communistic society of the present day. He taught: "Let your hand be always open to the unfortunate." "When the poor man knocks at your door, take him in and administer to his wants, for the poor are the chosen of God." "Contemn riches and worldly honor." "There should be no disagreement between your lives and your doctrine." "Spend every day as though it were the last." "Much riches is a curse to the possessor." "A good, wise, and benevolent man can not be rich." "Money does not satisfy the love of gain, but only stimulates it." "He who gives to the needy, loses nothing himself." "Above all things, cultivate love for your neighbor."

So far in this world's history communism has gained no foothold in any community, except as identified with some particular religious creed.

Therefore, for successful communism or socialism, we must look to the body of religious enthusiasts. In proof of this, the history of the career of Chrishna, the Christ of the Hindoo Buddhist, was cited. We find the same thing exemplified in the writings of the Christian bible. Moses, in the laws he promulgated for the government of his people, was communistic, as we plainly read in the books of Leviticus and Deuteronomy. Evidently Moses took into consideration the fact that human nature—the same then as to-day—was so constituted, that, starting out with an equal division of property for all the people, the year of Jubilee must be established in order to restore to the people their rightful possessions; that the land which, from force of circumstances, had passed from the original occupants into the hands of the more thrifty, and the wealthy, must be re-divided at least once in fifty years, in order to restore the equilibrium; and so it came about that Moses gave out his decree to the people that, "Ye shall hallow the fiftieth year and proclaim liberty throughout all the land unto all the inhabitants thereof : it shall be a jubilee unto you; and ye shall return every man unto his possession—the land shall not be sold forever."

Moses sought to prevent extreme poverty by compelling the wealthy to share their riches with their less fortunate neighbors; this was the civil law of the land, but consecrated by religion, and only held in force so long as the religion of Moses was predominant and governed the people. In time, this form of communism failed, and wholly because of the failure of the Jews to remain steadfast in the faith of their fathers. The great desire for emolument and wealth took firm possession of the people to the entire exclusion of the tenets promulgated by Moses, and notwithstanding the denunciations heaped upon them by that greatest of all socialists, the prophet Isaiah, whose thunder tones must have stung to the quick those who sought to "grind the faces of the poor," they did not however cease to "join house to house and field to field," unmindful of Isaiah's cry "that there be no place left in the land ! "

But in what direction did Isaiah look for relief from the oppression of the wealthy? Was it not in the appearance of a king, the Messiah, who would banish from the face of the earth all injustice and selfishness, and restore to the people of God the land of their fathers? And as the state of society grew ever worse, the poor growing poorer and the oppressed more oppressed, we find their champions in Jeremiah and Ezekiel, who joined with Isaiah in proclaiming words of most bitter denunciation of the avarice of the wealthy, and in the promise of a deliverance from all their woes for those who should remain steadfast in the faith.

And when the deliverer came in the person of Christ, do we not find him preaching "the Gospel to the poor" and proclaiming "deliverance to the captives ? " Are not the rich most unmercifully denounced by him and the poor blessed? Is not his injunction to the rich young man the very keynote of communism?—"Go and sell that thou hast, and give to the poor, and thou shalt have treasure in heaven: and come and follow me." And i i all his teachings, do we not see ever uppermost the fundamental idea of a state of society where perfect equality of property shall be enjoyed alike by all the earth? And this same form of communism has been kept alive by the teachings of the church, in a greater or less degree as it has conformed to the teachings of Christ.

The early fathers of the church stigmatized the accumulation of riches as no better than robbery. St. Jerome and St. Basil denounced in no mild terms the accumulation of wealth. They declared that "riches is robbery," and sought with all their power to turn the people from such selfish pursuits.

And so through all the dark ages, and during all the struggle of individuals for supremacy, the strong man overpowering the weak, creating himself a lord, regarding the weak as but an underling—a serf—and installed by him as a toiler by the sweat of whose brow the labor was performed that enabled him to exist in idleness and luxury; we find the lackey constantly smarting from his wounds, but seemingly powerless to rise above his surroundings, or to improve his condition.

And how can we expect any other state of affairs in this world so long as human nature remains the same? True, the refining influence of the Christian religion has done much to ameliorate the condition of mankind; but aside from a few communistic societies, of which probably that of the Shakers is to-day the most perfect type we have, do we find the communistic doctrine as established by Christ anywhere practiced or taught in our churches?

All the talk of the government assuming the functions of commerce now enjoyed by corporations and individuals, of making one universal salaried rate for all, is chimerical in the extreme. The desire for independent individualism was what led the first settlers to these western shores, and that trait of human nature is just as strong in man to-day as then. And until an entirely different race of human beings, wholly devoid of the peculiar characteristics which are now such prominent features, shall have become inhabitants of our land, need we expect any great change in our social economy.

We find in the ancient sect of Essenes, a communistic society of Christians, who, if we may believe the words of that Roman naturalist and author, Pliny, have existed for thousands of ages. And furthermore, is it not surpassingly strange that a sect whose exemplary virtues commanded the unbounded admiration of even the Greeks and Romans, and whose doctrines and practices were so strikingly similar to the teachings of Christ, should be so little known among intelligent Christians?

Perhaps this may be accounted for on the ground that Evangelical Christians seem to have been extremely anxious to hide every appearance of similarity between Essenism and Christianity, lest the popular mind become imbued with the idea that Christianity sprang from Essenism. On the other hand, it is plain that the Rationalists have sought to make most prominent every feature of resemblance between the two as a proof that Christianity is but the offspring of Essenism. At any rate, this is the idea that an unbiased mind will be likely to have after a perusal of the religious histories of the evangelical churches and the popular encyclopædias on this subject. Therefore we are led to seek our information regarding this most remarkable sect from the fountain source from which all the reliable information we have of this people originally came.

The first mention we have of the existence of the Essenes is in the days of Jonathan, the Maccabean, one hundred and sixty-six years before Christ. We find this in the "Antiquities" of the Jewish historian, Flavius Josephus, xiii., 5–8. The next mention of them is by the same historian in his "Jewish War," 1-3 sec. 5 ; Antiq. xiii., sec. 2, in the reign of Aristobulus I., 106 B. C. It will be remembered that Josephus was born in Jerusalem about 37 A. D. He wrote in Greek, and improved every opportunity to impress upon the Greeks and Romans that every phase and sect of Judaism had its counterpart in all the different systems of Greek and Roman philosophy.

Philo, who was born in Alexandria somewhere between the years 20 and 1 B. C., has given us two accounts of the Essenes ; one in his treatise : "Every Virtuous Man is Free," and the other, his "Apology for the Jews." However, as during his whole life he resided in Alexandria, his information respecting the Essenes must have been gathered from others. He attributes the foundation of the order to Moses.

We next read of the Essenes in Pliny's "Natural History," book v., chap. xvii. The author, Caius Plinius Secundus, was born in Rome, A. D. 23, and died in the year 79. He asserts that, without a single addition by birth, incredible as this may appear, the Essenes have prolonged their existence for thousands of ages. The next in order of time is the testimony of Josephus, in his history of the "Jewish Wars," book ii., chap. viii., sec. 2-13 ; also Antiq., book viii., chap v., sec. 9, and book xv., chap. x., sec. 4, etc.

Then we next find an account of the Essenes in the "Polyhistor," a geographical compendium ; the author of which, Caius Julius Solinus, flourished about the year 238, but it is plain that what he says of them in chap. xxxv., sec. 7–10, is taken from Pliny.

The next we read of the Essenes is in the treatise of the celebrated Greek philosopher, and antichristian writer, Porphyry, who was born about the year 233 and died about 305. In his work "On the Abstinence from Animal Food" (Lugduni ap Morillon, 1620, p. 381,) he gives an account of the Essenes, but as he tells us, taken from Josephus, although he enlarges somewhat on what we find in Josephus in relation to the sect. Porphyry, Solinus and Pliny were greatly prejudiced gainst the Jews and seldom granted them justice in the matter of their religion even when conversant with the inward workings of it. The account of the Essenes which we have in the ecclesiastical history of Pamphili Eusebius, the Bishop of Cesarea, who was born about the year 270, and died about 338, is copied from Philo.

The foregoing named authorities are all the witnesses that are now extant who can give us any information regarding the character of this most ancient people who originated at a date long ages ago, but precisely when, it is now impossible to tell. Josephus says that they have existed "ever since the ancient time of the fathers."

The Christian writer, Epiphanius, drew largely upon his imagination in relation to this people, as have all others down to more recent times who have departed in any material degree from the following testimony as found in the works we have mentioned, and which have been compiled and embodied in an essay reprinted from the transactions of the Literary and Philosophical Society of Liverpool, entitled "The Essenes: their History and Doctrines," by Christian D. Ginsburg, L. L. D., London, 1861. The doctrines and practices of the Essenes were as follows: The law of God, as expounded by Moses, was held in the utmost veneration by them, and indeed, to such an extent was this carried, that they visited with capital punishment any of their number who blasphemed the name of Moses, the great law-giver. Their highest aim was to attain that spiritual intercourse with God which would enable them to prophesy, perform miracles and miraculous cures, and so, become like Elias, the forerunner of the Messiah. This they regarded as the last stage of perfection on this earth, and which could only be reached by a gradual growth in holiness and a strict observance of all the commandments, and the Levitical laws of purity as contained in the Pentateuch; mortifying the flesh and the lusts thereof; being meek and lowly in spirit, inasmuch as this would bring them into closer communion with God. They regarded the taking of oaths as a desecration. Their communication was yea, yea; nay, nay, and whatever was more than this, came from evil. Imbued with this manner of thought as their aim in life, the Essenes withdrew themselves altogether from the society of the Jews and formed a separate community, with the fundamental idea, that to be pure, they must live apart from the world, since contact with any one who did not practice these laws, rendered them impure. It was this same idea of purity that impelled them to abstain from marriage, which was regarded by them as defiling. They sought to carry out the very letter of the law as given in Leviticus, chap. xv., 16-33; Exodus, chap. xix., 15, believing that it was only by living the life of a celibate that they could be pure. In 1 Corinthians, chap. vii., 5-9, we find St. Paul teaching this same doctrine. There were, however, some weak brethren, even among the Essenes, who could not be like the angels in heaven, neither marrying nor are given in marriage, and these were allowed to take unto themselves wives, but in consequence of it were debarred from advancing to the highest orders of the brotherhood, and had, moreover, to observe laws especially enacted for the married brethren and sisters.

Each person upon entering the order was required to deposit in the general treasury all he possessed, from which the wants of the whole community were supplied; therefore all things were held in common by them; there were neither rich nor poor in their community; no masters nor servants. They lived peaceably with all men: reprobated slavery and war, and would not even manufacture any martial instruments. They were governed by a president who was elected by the whole body, and who also acted as the judge of the community. Trials were conducted by a jury composed of a majority of the community, or of at least a hundred members, who were required to render a unanimous verdict. The brother who was found guilty of walking disorderly, was excommunicated, yet not regarded as an enemy, but admonished as a brother, and was received back after due repentance.

As it was contrary to the laws of Levitical purity to purchase anything from one not practicing those laws, the Essenes were obliged to supply themselves from their own resources, with all of their wants, each one in the community willingly took his share of the work in the department in which he most excelled. Some tilled the ground, others tended the flocks and engaged in the rearing of bees; some prepared the food, while others made their articles of dress; some were physicians, and some instructors of the young; whilst all of them devoted certain hours to studying the mysteries of nature and revelation, and of the celestial hierarchy. They arose in the morning before the sun, and never talked about any worldly matters until they had all assembled together, then with their faces turned toward the rising sun, they sang their national hymn of praise to God for the renewal of the light of day. This done, each betook himself to his regular daily employment, according as the overseers might direct. At the fifth hour (eleven o'clock in the forenoon,) all assembled together for a baptism in cold water, donned their white garments, the symbol of purity, and then made their way to the refectory for their noonday meal, entering with as much solemnity as if it were the temple.

The meal was a very common one, and each member took his seat according to the order of his age. The bakers and cooks then placed before each one a small loaf of bread and a dish of the most simple food, consisting chiefly of vegetables, as they ate very little animal flesh. After a blessing by the priest, they partook of the repast in a mysterious silence during the entire meal, which seemed to partake of a sacrament, and perhaps designed by them as a substitute for the sacrifices which they refused to offer in the temple. The priest terminated the meal by again offering thanks to the Bountiful Supplier of all our wants, which was the sign of dismissal. Thereupon all withdrew, laid aside their white and sacred garments, resumed their working clothes, and repaired to their several occupations until evening, when they returned as before to another common meal.

Although everything was done by direction of the overseers, and all payments and presents came from the hands of the stewards, yet in two things they were at perfect liberty to act as they pleased. They could relieve the distressed with as much money as they thought proper, and could manifest their compassion for those who were not of the brotherhood as much as they pleased. Such was their manner of life during the week days.

The Sabbath was observed by them with the utmost rigor, and they regarded even the removal of a vessel as labor and a desecration of the holy day. Ten persons constituted a complete and legal number for divine worship in their synagogue. In the presence of such an assembly, an Essene would never spit, and upon no occasion would he spit to his right hand.

They had no ordained ministers whose exclusive right it was to conduct the service; any one who liked could read from their sacred books, whilst another, perhaps with more experience in spiritual matters, expounded what was read. The distinctive ordinances of the brotherhood, as well as the mysteries connected with the Tetragrammaton and the angelic worlds were the prominent topics of Sabbatic instruction. Every investigation into the causes of the phenomena, both of mind and matter, was strictly forbidden, because the study of logic and metaphysics was regarded as injurious to a devotional life.

Celibacy being the rule of Essenism, they looked to the Jewish community at large for recruits with which to fill the ranks of the brotherhood. They preferred the taking of children, whom they educated most carefully, teaching them the practices of the order. Every adult candidate was required to pass through a novitiate of two stages, extending for the term of three years, before he could be fully admitted into the order. At the very outset he was required to cast all of his possessions into the common treasury. He then received a copy of the regulations of the brotherhood, also a spade, in accordance with the command in Deuteronomy xxiii., 12–14, also an apron and a white robe, as a symbol of purity, to be worn at his meal. During the whole of this period he was but an outsider, never being admitted to the common meals, yet obliged to observe some of the ascetic rules of the society. If the candidate properly acquitted himself during this probationary period, he was, at the end of his term, admitted into the second stage of his installment, lasting for two years, and was then known as an "approacher." During this period he was admitted to a closer fellowship with the brotherhood, and shared in their lustral rites; still he was not admitted to their common meals, nor to any office. If he passed satisfactorily through this second stage of his probation, the "approacher" became an "associate," or a full member of the society. But before he was made a homiletic, he must bind himself by a most solemn oath (this being the only occasion an Essene ever takes an oath) to observe three things: 1st, love to God; 2d, merciful justice towards all men; honoring no man as master; avoiding the wicked;

helping the righteous; being faithful to every man, and especially towards rulers, for without God no one comes to be a ruler; 3rd, purity of character, which implied humility, love of truth, hatred of falsehood, strict secrecy towards outsiders, that the sacred doctrines be not divulged to any one, and perfect openness with the members of the order; and, finally, carefully to preserve the books belonging to their sect, and the names of the angels, or the mysteries connected with the Tetragrammaton, and the other names of God and the angels, comprised in the theosophy, as well as with the cosmogony which also played so important a part among the Jewish mystics and the Kabbalists.

The three sections of the novitiate were subdivided into four orders, distinguished from each other by superior holiness; and so marked and serious were these distinctions, that if one belonging to a higher degree of purity touch one of a lower order, however far advanced he might be before he was received into the full order and had taken the oath, the one of the higher order immediately became impure, and could only regain his purity by lustrations.

From the beginning of the novitiate to the time of his achievement of the highest spiritual state, there were eight different stages which marked the gradual growth in holiness.

The first stage attained after receiving the white apron, was the outward, or bodily purity, by baptism. That of the second, related to abstinence from connubial intercourse. The third, that of inward or spiritual purity; fourth, to the banishing of all anger and malice, and the cultivation of a meek and lowly spirit; fifth, to the culminating point of holiness. From this summit of holiness he passed to the sixth stage, to that of the temple of the Holy Spirit, and could prophesy. At the seventh stage, he was enabled to perform miraculous cures, and to raise the dead. On arriving at the eighth and last stage, he reached to the position of Elias—the forerunner of the Messiah.

From the fact that Josephus says the Essenes "lived the same kind of life which, among the Greeks, has been ordered by Pythagoras," some writers assert that Essenism is the offspring of Pythagorism. The most able champion for this view is Zeller, the author of the "History of Philosophy." But the differences between the two are quite marked. First, the Pythagoreans were essentially polytheists; the Essenes, real monotheistic Jews, and worshipers of the Holy One of Israel; second, the Pythagoreans clustered around Pythagoras as the center of their spiritual and intellectual life; the Essenes regarding the inspired scriptures as their sole source of spiritual life; thirdly, the Pythagoreans favored matrimony, and we are told that Pythagoras himself had a wife and children; whilst the Essenes regarded the marriage state as one of impurity, and that those in it could never attain to the high standard of spiritual happiness and purity of the celibate.

CHAPTER I.

SHAKERISM IN ENGLAND.

THERE is at the present day a society of Christians found, we are told, now only in America, which have many of the characteristics of the Essenes. Indeed, they have so many features in common, one is almost led to think that the United Society of Believers, called Shakers, are but the lineal descendants of the Essenes.

Time brings its changes in every department of life, and so we look for it in religious as well as in secular affairs. And we find very many marked changes in the evangelical doctrines that are promulgated from the pulpits of our churches to-day from that of even a quarter of a century ago. What changes then may we expect to find when measured by the lapse of hundreds of centuries? Certainly no less than now appears between the tenets of the Essenes of three thousand years ago and their counterpart of to-day, the American Shakers, in this the nineteenth century.

Christ and his apostles were Essenes in many of the features of the religion which they taught. Equally true is this of the Society of Shakers. And neither do we find any other religious sect so closely following the teachings of the Essenes, and of Christ and his apostles, as do the Shakers. It can truthfully be said of them that they have left the follies and frivolities of life to follow the teachings of Christ. And still, paradoxical as it may seem to many, the Shakers do not believe that Christ is God, nor the son of God, only as he was the first-born son into the new creation—the heavenly Jerusalem; the eldest brother of other sons of God, yet to be born into the new creation. They declare that they "love him only for his works' sake," and, because in "Jesus alone were all the characteristics of a perfect Christian."

But who are the Shakers? And what is Shakerism? The first question is easily answered, as most of us, at one time or another, have met with some of the Brethren and Sisters of "this peculiar people," dressed in the singular garb by which they have been known to the world for upwards of a century. The Brethren in their drab suits and light drab hats; the Sisters in their plain dresses, entirely devoid of trimming of any kind, with a white or colored silk kerchief over their shoulders, the head and face quite concealed by a plain Quaker bonnet,—this constituted to the average mind, about all there was of Shakerism a quarter of a century ago.

But what is this Shakerism which has given a century's proof, in this country, as being one of the most successful forms of communism ever devised.

There has ever been a time in the history of nations when a body of religious enthusiasts have existed analogous, in some measure, to our American Shakers. They may be found in the followers of Chrishna Zeus in Hindostan, 2500 years B. C. ; of Zulis, or Zhulis, in Egypt, 1700 years B. C. ; of Crite in Chaldea, 1200 years B. C, ; of Atys in Phrygia, 1170 years B. C. ; of Thammuz in Syria, 1160 years B. C. ; of Hesus in Gaul, 834 years B. C. ; of Baal, "the only begotten of God," in Phœnicia, and of Indra in Thibet, and of Bali, or Bel, in Asia, 725 years B. C. ; of Mithra in Persia, 600 years B. C. ; of Budha Sakia in India, 590 years B. C. : of Quexalcote in Mexico, 587 years B. C. ; of Prometheus in Caucasus, 547 years B. C. ; of Quirinus in Rome, 506 years B. C. ; all of whom, history tells us, were crucified as "sons of the Most High," and saviors of the world.

Shakerism is Spiritualism, and to use their own words, "the most radical Spiritualists of our day."

And they further declare ; "We are thoroughly convinced of spirit communication and interpositions, spirit guidance and obsession. Our Spiritualism has permitted us to converse, face to face, with individuals once mortals, some of whom we well knew, and with others born before the flood. All spiritual phenomena commonly occurring in the world had an inauguration among us, long before the Rochester rappings. By our Spiritualism we are become confirmed infidels to the foolish *bodily resurrection theory;* to the untrue and disappointing *atonement doctrine;* to the monstrous *trinity* scheme ; to the cruel *predestination* belief, and to all the man-made creeds of the *popular* churches professing Christianity. We are sure these theories are untrue, and we have had hundreds of testimonies from those who, when in the body, were as firm in the belief of their verity as any can be now, but who were bitterly disappointed on arrival in the spirit world." *

Shakerism is a prominent type of Christian communism—a "community of goods," which has never been more perfectly accomplished than by the Shakers. They are Christian celibates, practicing all the virtues and avoiding all the vices incident to mankind, and have flourished in this country with remarkable success for more than a century. Landing in America from England in 1774, a little band of but nine individuals, virtually without "purse or scrip," but now with a membership of above two thousand persons, and landed possessions of more than sixty thousand acres of excellent farming lands, including sixteen villages of house, mill and other manufacturing property ; these rank them as a most thrifty people. They are strictly temperate in all things, and offer no worldly inducements for individuals to join their order. Applicants must come, if they come at all, of their own volition, anxious to embrace Shakerism because of its godliness : and before one would be admitted as one of their fraternity, they would be asked this as one of the first questions : "What is your motive in wishing to join

---

* "Plain Talks Concerning the Shakers," page 12.

us?" If the answer comes, as it must in the end to prove efficacious; "I am sick of sin, and want salvation from it!" And where this is apparent, they are never anxious to know if the individual is rich or poor, but prefer the latter, "with only the clothes commonly in the possession of moral, cleanly people, rather than to admit any for other reasons, though they had the wealth of an Astor." And, further, any one seeking admission as a member, is required, ere they have any encouragement at all, "to settle, as far as possible, all debts and contracts to the satisfaction of creditors;" and then their rule is: "If candid seekers after salvation come to us, we neither accept them nor reject them; we *admit* them, leaving the spirit of goodness to decide as to their sincerity; to bless their efforts, if sincere, or to make them very dissatisfied if hypocritical. After becoming thoroughly acquainted with our principles, we ask individuals to give evidence of their sincerity by an honest confession of their sins, as committed against their own light, or conscience, to the spirit of God, as they now receive it and this act of contrition is to be in prayer before a witness of their own sex. We are led to believe by accepting the testimony of Jesus the Christ that without an honest confession to God, there is no remission for sin, and this cannot be done only as the individual walks in the light of life by putting away the influences of the world and by putting on the life of Christ. It often takes years for an individual to complete this work of *thorough confession and repentance*; but upon this more than aught else, depends their success as permanent and happy members." *

The Shakers are quite indifferent as to the religious belief of their incoming members. They say to all such: "We do not lay so much stress upon what you may have believed, whether it be concerning a trinity or a duality in Deity, only let no God be an interference to the principle of strictest discipline of purity. Incline, if you choose to predestination, only regard it as established that you were predestined as a Christian, to be a follower of Jesus in virginity of life and thought. Believe, if you please, in Jesus as an atonement, and continue to do so if you prefer, but also assure us that at-one-ment with Christ, is to live free and apart from fleshly lusts and worldly ambitions, and to pattern your life by the Christian model. We are not concerned about your metaphysics, your materialism, nor spiritualism, but we ask you to square your life by him whose life was without blemish." †

To the world they say: "When all things of earth, man-made creeds, worldly pleasures, and carnal vanities—fail to yield that needed peace and rest to weary spirits, turn to your nearest and dearest friends—the Shakers." ‡

About the year 1706, a type of religionists, claiming to have direct communion with the spirit world, made much commotion in England. They were first heard of in France, about 1689, and as the outcome from the revo-

---

* "Plain Talks Concerning the Shakers," page 20.   †Ibid.
‡ "Plain Talks concerning the Shakers," page 22.

lutionists of Dauphine and Vivarais. Some of the number passed over into England in the beginning of the eighteenth century, and began to preach their peculiar doctrine to the populace of Manchester. Their efforts culminated in most remarkable religious revivals, which in time spread over the whole continent of Europe. Many converts to the new religion went into trances and prophesied that the end of all things was near at hand; and that the Scripture prophecies, concerning a "new heaven and a new earth," were about to be accomplished. They predicted the sure downfall and destruction of all false systems of religion, and the total annihilation of that anti-christian spirit which then held such extensive sway among the churches.

They spoke with great power and energy of spirit, warning the people to repent of their sins, and to lead new lives, and to make themselves ready for the "marriage feast of the Lamb," and a life in the new Jerusalem which was shortly to dawn upon them.

The powerful admonitions, coming from these religious fanatics, had an alarming effect upon the populace, who were taught that: "When all the false systems of human invention, all the deceitful and abominable works of man should be pulled down and destroyed, there would be but one Lord, one faith, one heart, and one voice among mankind; and that this would all be accomplished by spiritual influence acting through living mediums."*

As might be supposed, the effect of such preaching, coming to the ears of the established churches and clergy, aroused a feeling of disquietude and alarm among them which shortly took the form of persecution against the "fanatics," as the spiritualists were called. Many of them were imprisoned on trumped-up charges, others banished, but the seed had been sown, not to be eradicated, and to a greater or less extent the "new religion" continued for the space of forty years, when a little band of enthusiasts, under the lead of James Wardley, a powerful and impressive speaker of the Quaker denomination, and a resident of Manchester, England, formed themselves into a society at Bolton, near Manchester. Jane Wardley, the wife of James, was exceedingly gifted as his assistant, and the little band prospered, so that in due time, additional meetings were held regularly in Manchester, and other adjoining towns. This society was of the extreme order of Spiritualists. They "held to no special forms, nor adopted any creed, either as a rule of faith, or as an order of worship," but believed that God manifested Himself to honest, prayerful souls, gave themselves to be actuated by, led and guided, entirely by the spirit of divinity, moving and governing their every action.

In their religious meetings, silence for a time might reign supreme; then as the spirit of some departed soul, which, mayhap, had long before the Flood left this world, sought out some devout brother or sister of that silent gathering, as a medium of communication, through which to testify of the joys of that life beyond the tomb, the chosen one would be seized with a vi-

---

*"Shaker Compendium" 3rd edition, page 20.

olent trembling, and a mighty agitation of body and limbs. Then would the spirit be moved throughout the entire congregation of worshipers to such a degree that shouting, singing, and leaping for joy, they would swiftly pass and re-pass each other, like reeds shaken in a mighty wind. Then, as if acted upon by one all-pervading impulse, silence would fall, like the stillness of death, upon the worshipers, while the chosen one would recite, to their anxious listeners, the spirit message of love or warning.

Such strange actions, in the eyes of the curious and ungodly, were regarded with derision, and very soon the band of spirit worshipers were known by the appellation of "Shaking Quakers," or, for short, "Shakers," which latter name was adopted by the fraternity as their cognomen.

CHAPTER II.

MOTHER ANN LEE.

OF the congregation of the little society of Shaking Quakers at Manchester, over which James and Jane Wardley were the head, was a family of the name of Lee. They were poor in this world's goods, as, indeed, were almost all the members of Mr. Wardley's society. The father of this family, John Lee, was a sturdy blacksmith in Manchester, and followed his trade industriously. He had the reputation of strict honesty in all his dealings with those who gave him patronage. He was a moral man, and brought up his family of five sons and three daughters as well as his very limited circumstances would permit. At a very early age, the children were all placed out at work to earn their pittance to add to the scanty income of the father in the maintenance of the family.

Of the children, there was a daughter by the name of Ann, who, in after years, made a most notable excitement in the Shaker community, of which she became the head and front—indeed, the very foundation stone of American Shakerism.

Ann Lee was born in a house standing in what is now known as Todd street, in Manchester, on the 29th of February, 1736. She at first found employment, when but a mere child, in a cotton factory, where she was placed by her parents. Subsequently she left this situation for a position in a hat factory, as a cutter of hatters' fur; and still later on we find her as a cook in a hospital in Manchester. In the several positions which she filled, in childhood and youth, and at a more advanced age, she gave good satisfaction to her employers; and to all with whom she came in contact, she is said to have been kind and complaisant.

As a child, she was bright, but lacking in the refinements of education, and still she was above the average of her associates in intelligence, notwithstanding she could neither read nor write. Very early in life she showed a remaikable religious tendency of mind, and was more inclined to listen to the conversation of her elders on that subject than to engage in play with her comrades. At about the age of fourteen or fifteen, she began to have more than a special interest in the meetings held by Mr. Wardley, and she often spoke to her mother of her "heavenly visions," and of her "great tribulation of soul" over the depravity of human nature; and to such an extent was she possessed of these expressed experiences, that she came to be considered by her friends and relatives a monomaniac on the subject of religion.

As time passed on, she made the acquaintance of a young man of the name of Abraham Stanley, a village blacksmith, towards whom she became very friendly. Her relatives became over-anxious to bring about a match between the two, with the idea, that, as a wife and mother, she might be brought out of that extraordinary state of excitation into which her mind had drifted. Expressing freely her great repugnance to matrimonial alliances, even to the extent of saying that it was a carnal sin for men and women to cohabit as husband and wife; that Christ's example set for his followers must be her law; that as he mortified all fleshly lusts by rejecting the temptations of Satan and living the life of a celibate, so must she: therefore they found it no easy task to bring her over to their way of thinking, notwithstanding she was ardently importuned by young Stanley, for whom she had great respect, if not maidenly affection. However, as the constant falling of a drop of water makes its impression on the hardest stone, so she found her resolutions weakening under the pressure brought to bear upon her, until at last she very reluctantly consented to the union, and they were united in the bonds of matrimony. They took up their residence in her father's house. In time four children were born to them, but all died in their infancy. Perhaps it was the loss of her children which often brought back with increasing force the convictions of her youth and maidenhood. Be that as it may, she was often noticed as being under a great depression of spirits—"a fearful conviction of sin," as she herself expressed it, and from which she could "obtain no relief day nor night." She was often known to spend the entire night in "laboring and crying to God to open some way of salvation."*

In 1758, when she had arrived at the twenty-third year of her age, she decided to consummate what for a long time she had in her mind to do, which was to unite herself with Mr. Wardley's society. At this date, she was, in personal appearance, a well-proportioned, light-complexioned woman; rather stoutly built, but straight and regular in form and features; fair of face, with blue eyes full of expression; her hair brown, of a light chestnut hue; her glance keen and penetrating; her countenance mild, inspiring confidence and respect. By many she was looked upon as saintly

---

*Shaker Compendium, third edition, page 123.

and beautiful. Physically, she was the picture of health; mentally, she had no peer in the society into which she was baptized.

Here, at last, among this people, she found that rest for her soul, that protection from inclination to sin, which had for so long a period been the burden of her prayers. She at once took prominent rank in the society. Her years of fasting, her cries to God for deliverance from sin, were as messengers from heaven of her experiences which she related in her fervent appeals to her hearers in the little church of her adoption. Her testimonies as to personal visions, and the mysteries of the heavenly world sank deep into the hearts of the communicants of the church, opened their understanding, and encouraged their faith to continue in the work which they had begun. They fully believed in the open confession of every sin committed, and in the taking up of the cross against everything they felt to be evil.

For twelve years this society of shaking Quakers continued to prosper, with comparatively little interference or persecution. But it was as the dead calm before the mighty wind which was so soon to shake their superstructure to the very foundation.

Becoming emboldened by the apparent security from interference by the populace of Manchester, they boldly began an onslaught upon other forms of religion which they deemed "fraught with evil and damnable heresies." They proclaimed the second coming of Christ, and that it was nigh at hand; that soon would be experienced the downfall of antichrist, and the overthrow of the abominable creeds of religion that had foisted themselves upon a suffering people.

Their bold and aggressive warfare against every feature of sin was soon sorely felt by the ungodly, both in and outside of the churches. Their meetings excited public attention, even the churches and clergy were stirred to make open protest, and made formal opposition to the continuance of the meetings. Encouraged, if not openly sanctioned, by the latter, mobs congregated with the avowed purpose of suppressing the "heretics" at any cost. Thus perilous times fell upon the "faithful," and very many were put in jeopardy of their lives.

Ann Lee and her associates were frequently arrested and thrown into prison. On one occasion she was forcibly dragged out of the meeting and cast into a prison in Manchester, and placed in a cell so small that she could not recline at full length. Here she was kept without food for fourteen days, and not once during that time was the door of her cell opened. Food was, however, conveyed to her by a lad of nineteen, by the name of James Whittaker, whom Ann had brought up from his boyhood. He succeeded in supplying her secretly with a mixture of wine and milk by inserting the stem of a tobacco pipe through the key-hole of the cell door. At the end of her term of imprisonment, the turnkey unlocked the door of her cell with the glad expectation of finding her dead from starvation. Judge, then, of his astonishment "to see her depart, looking just as well as when she entered." *

It was on this occasion that "the dark and dismal cell became the illuminated abode of spiritual life and joy," when "she saw Jesus Christ in open vision, who revealed to her the most astounding views and divine manifestations of truth, in which she had a perfect and clear insight of the mystery of iniquity, the root and foundation of all human depravity, and of the very act of transgression committed by Adam and Eve in the garden of Eden.† In this vision she saw what "was the only possible and effectual remedy and means of salvation"—the "taking up of the complete cross against the lusts of generation." ‡ In substance, Ann's testimony was that Christ never taught that the system of matrimony was a part of the heavenly abode, but, on the contrary, that in his "Father's house of many mansions, there was neither marrying nor giving in marriage," and that Christ came to prepare the people of earth for this blissful abode, and himself set the example, in all things, which he would have them follow. Ann saw that "in the old man, the first Adam, *the multiplier*, all die." For was it not in holy writ: "If ye live after the flesh, ye shall die." But, in "the new man, the Christ, the second Adam, the celibate, all are made alive." It was made clear to her that there were "two creations, old and new. Adam, the first, the husband of Eve, inaugurated the old creation, with marriage and generation as its basic law. Jesus, the Christ, inaugurated the new creation, with virgin purity and regeneration as its fundamental law. The first Adam, a sower of the world; the second Adam, the reaper." §

On emerging from the prison, she imparted to the society this revelation made known to her by the heavenly vision, and the society accepted it as revealed light from God, and from that time forth "acknowledged her as the first visible leader of the Church of God upon the earth," ‖ and readily accepted her as their spiritual mother in Christ, and ever after was regarded by them "as Mother Ann Lee." ¶ In point of fact, they considered this manifestation as the *actual second coming of* Christ, through the head of their Church, Mother Ann Lee. "Thus they became one, and the marriage of the Lamb and Bride was completed by God himself, and thus ended the mystery of the second coming of Christ." ** And so the community of Shakers no more look for a second coming of Christ, because he has already appeared through Mother Ann.

In the biographical sketch of Ann Lee in the "Shaker Compendium," we

---

* "Shaker Compendium," third edition, page 133.
† "The Life and Gospel Experience of Mother Ann Lee," page 5, and "Shaker Compendium," third edition, page 128.
‡ "Shaker Compendium," third edition, page 128.   § "Sketches of Shakerism," page 12.
‖ "Life and Gospel Experience of Mother Ann Lee," page 6.
¶ "Life and Gospel Experience of Mother Ann Lee," page 6.
** From a recently published sermon preached by H. L. Eads, bishop of the Shakers at South Union, Ky.

find many instances of her "miraculous deliverance" from danger and death. Once, when seized by a mob who were in the act of stoning her to death, she received deliverance at the hands of a nobleman who had been "wrought upon in his mind, and urged by his feelings to go, but where, or for what cause, he did not know."* Again, when in the hands of a mob, who were seeking to bind her with ropes, an invisible power stayed their hands. And again, when she was accused of blasphemy, and was told that her tongue should be bored through with a hot iron and her cheek branded, and as preliminary to the proceeding she was taken before four ministers of the Established Church, with a view of obtaining judgment against her, these she confounded by speaking, as they declared, "for four hours, in seventy-two different tongues," which "had the effect of causing them to advise the mob not to molest her." This so enraged them, that they determined to stone her to death, " as a blasphemer." Accordingly, to make thorough work of it, they took Ann and her brother William, James and Daniel Whittaker, into a valley outside the town, with that intent. But their hands were withheld, they "could not hit any of them," and "falling into a contention among themselves, they abandoned their wicked design.†

Ann's last imprisonment in England was for "Sabbath breaking." The allegation was, that "dancing, shouting and shaking in the worship of God on the Sabbath day was profaning the Sabbath." Spies were stationed in the street near their place of meeting, under the pretence of preventing gatherings of the people who were profaning the Lord's day. On that morning, the "believers" assembled at the house of John Lee, the blacksmith and the father of Ann, and began their worship as usual. The spies gave the alarm, and a mob was soon raised, headed by the principal Warden in Manchester. "They surrounded the house, burst open the doors, seized without ceremony the worshipers, and hurried them away to the stone prison, where they placed them in close confinement. The company were released the next morning, with the exception of Mother Ann and John Lee, who were removed to another place of confinement and held as prisoners for several weeks."‡

CHAPTER III.

EMBARKATION FOR AMERICA—SETTLEMENT IN NISKEYUNA.

IN the spring of the year 1774, Mother Ann Lee imparted to her congregation a "special revelation from heaven," in which she was directed to select

---

*"Shaker Compendium," third edition, p. 134.   † *Ibid* p. 135.
‡ "Life and Gospel Experience of Mother Ann Lee," pp. 6 and 7.

a chosen few and repair across the wide waters to a people of God. Her vision was of a large tree with outstretching branches, every leaf of which shone with the brightness of a burning torch, indicating the church of Christ yet to be established in the land of America. Though she was to go as a stranger to that far-distant shore, the forms and features of some of those whom she was to meet were made so clear to her that she declared she would recognize them upon her arrival.

Eight of the congregation were selected to accompany Mother Ann on her mission to America. Passage was secured with Captain Smith on the ship Mariah bound from Liverpool for New York, and on the 19th of May, 1774, Mother Ann, Abraham Stanley, (her husband,) William Lee (her brother,) Nancy Lee (her niece,) James Whittaker, John Hocknell and his son Richard, James Shepherd, and Mary Partington embarked for America. Each member of this religious band had previously received special spiritual manifestations from the other world, and this step taken, was, as they claimed, solely by the direction of spirits.

With the departure of this little band, Shakerism soon ceased to exist in England, and was never afterwards revived. The life and soul of the institution departed with Mother Ann, who was to establish in the new world a strange religion, and found a society of Communism, the marvel of the world.

Once on board the ship, the Shakers sought to worship God after their peculiar manner of marching or dancing, singing, and shaking, which greatly displeased Captain Smith, who sought to repress "such goings on" on board his ship. Failing to suppress by mild measures what he regarded as one of the worst features of blasphemy, he threatened to place the culprits in irons, and if that brought no reform, to cast them into the sea. But the Shakers knew no fear, and whenever "moved upon by the spirit," they went forth in song and dance to their worship as usual.

At last the greatly enraged captain proceeded to carry out at least a part of his threat. This was during a storm, when the waves were running high and the wind blowing a gale; but before he could make ready to execute it, there came a cry from below that the ship had sprung aleak and the water making rapidly in the hold. The crew sprang to the pumps, which were immediately put into use. Still the water gained very fast, and it looked as though all would be lost. Then came Mother Ann to the rescue, proclaiming to the frightened captain and crew that all would go well with them, for two angels from the spirit world had appeared to her announcing the perfect safety of the ship and all on board. The last proved true, for the cause of the leak was ascertained to be the starting of a plank, which was made secure, and the ship rode safely into New York harbor August 6, 1774.

About a year after the arrival of the company in New York, Abraham Stanley, who was not in sympathy with that measure of holiness which marked the life of Mother Ann, and failing in his attempts to induce her to change her pronounced views on the subject of celibacy, he left the order and took up with the society of another woman, thus dissolving the marriage ties that bound him to Mother Ann.

Until 1776, the Society of Believers remained in the vicinity of New York city, when in this year one of the Brothers, John Hocknell, who was possessed of considerable means, made a purchase of a section of land seven miles out from the town of Albany, in a wilderness called Niskeyuna, but now known as Watervliet, N. Y. Here for about three years and a half the Believers lived the life of celibates in comparative seclusion, holding everything in common, and toiling diligently in making improvements in their houses and lands, and providing a comfortable subsistence for themselves and the influx from the outer world which Mother Ann preached would come, and they felt would soon swell their numbers greatly.

In 1779, a remarkable religious revival commenced in the adjoining town of New Lebanon and adjacent places. Converts proclaimed special gifts of visions and made prophecies. The excitement partook of a spiritualistic nature ; mediums fell into trances, from which they announced that the second coming of Christ was at their very doors. Fired by their burning words of frenzy, "Seek and ye shall find ; knock, and it shall be opened unto you !" proselytes began their search for the promised Savior, and were led to visit the little settlement of Shakers in the backwoods of Niskeyuna to see if the isolated band of foreigners gathered there knew aught of his appearance. The party was made up of the middle-aged and veterans, young men and maidens, and on their arrival at the log houses in the wilderness they found a warm reception as expected guests. Mother Ann greeted them as old friends—co-laborers with her in the cause to which she had devoted her life and energies. Notwithstanding many of the young visitors were betrothed to each other in marriage, "all of the company became disciples of Ann Lee, and remained faithful Believers through life." * They accepted the doctrine of celibacy and communism ; of the duality of God— that he is both male and female—for so "God created man ; in the likeness of God made he him ; male and female created he them, and called their name Adam." † For as Christ first came and was made manifest through Jesus, a man, revealing the Father in Christ and God, so was the scheme of salvation made perfect by his second coming through Ann, revealing the Mother in Christ and God. And so Mother Ann was regarded as the embodiment of the second coming of Christ ; and thus Shakerism became a fixed institution in the community, and the very first of the communistic societies to be established in America, and which has wondrously flourished during its existence of nearly a century and a quarter in our midst.

---

* "The Life and Gospel Experience of Mother Ann Lee," page 12.
† Genesis, chap. v., v. 1–2.

The Shakers came to America in most perilous times. The country was full of excitement on account of the Stamp acts imposed upon it by the British government. This culminated the following year in the Revolutionary War in the struggle for independence. Every person not expressing himself in full sympathy with the revolutionists, was regarded as a Tory and an enemy to the country. Naturally, the little band of Shaker foreigners was looked upon with disfavor; at first, no doubt, from their avowed expressions upon every occasion against the sinfulness of war, but later on fostered from the fact of their rapid growth in numbers. Soon they were accused of being unfriendly to the patriotic cause, and were arraigned before the commissioners at Albany, who required them to take the oath of allegiance. This they refused to do, on the ground that swearing was contrary to their faith—"Swear not at all" was a cardinal feature of their religion. Upon this refusal, David Darrow, Joseph Meacham and John Hocknell were imprisoned. This was soon followed by the incarceration of Hezekiah Hammond and Joel Pratt, and finally by that of Mother Ann, Mary Partington, William Lee, James Whittaker and Calvin Harlow. These comprised the entire Board of Elders and leaders in the Shaker faith. This was in the month of July, 1780. Soon after Mother Ann was taken from the prison and conveyed down the Hudson river, with the intention of banishing her to the British army; but as this was found to be impracticable at that time, she was lodged in the jail at Poughkeepsie. In December of the same year they were all set at liberty upon the order of the governor of New York, George Clinton, afterwards vice-president of the United States.

The society, instead of suffering loss by the incarceration of the leaders for six months, largely grew in numbers, and Mother Ann and the Elders returned to their homes finding their institution in a far more prosperous condition than ever before.

CHAPTER IV.

WATERVLIET—PROSELYTING—DEATH OF MOTHER ANN LEE.

AFTER the release of the imprisoned Shakers from the jails at Albany and Poughkeepsie, N. Y., by the order of Governor Clinton, in the month of December, 1780, they returned to their home in Niskeyuna, the name of which place was not long after changed to that of Watervliet. During their incarceration they were daily visited by kind friends, who not only sympathized with them in their affliction and ministered to their wants, but became deeply interested in the story of their new and strange religion; and so great was their interest, that, upon the release of the prisoners, they journeyed with them to their little settlement in the backwoods of Albany, and became converts to the Shaker faith.

The cramped condition in which these pioneers lived offered no inducement in the way of luxuries—in fact, they hardly had the comforts of life, everything was of the simplest and plainest, and they had but little wherewith to share with those who sought to join them. Therefore, all those who accepted the doctrine of Shakerism and joined forces with them, were led to take the step from a deep feeling of conviction that God had revealed Himself to them through his servant, Mother Ann, and that it was their bounden duty to devote their lives in the most sacred manner to the preaching of the new faith, and the gathering in of God's people for the millennium and the commencement of Christ's kingdom on earth, on the threshold of which they

felt they stood. To this end, and with this intent, the most of the new converts parted from the Elders at Niskeyuna, each going to his own home, with the avowed purpose of becoming a minister unto himself and the community in which he resided.

For the following three or four years the tidings of the new religion spread far and near, and very many embraced

The Ancient Church of the Shakers at New Lebanon, N. Y.

the faith. They were to be found in many of the towns in the States of Massachusetts, Connecticut, New Hampshire and Maine.

At first the near by Believers often visited the parent society at Watervliet, with the feeling that by frequent communication with the Elders and Mother Ann their faith would be more firmly established, and themselves better fitted to meet the scoffers among the world's people, who, through false reports, were doing much to undo the work of the faithful. This was called "visiting the church," and for a time continued; but, in 1781, Mother Ann, with the Elders at Watervliet, feeling that a greater degree of spiritual gift would be imparted to their followers if they were ministered to in their own homes, decided upon a visitation to the places and homes of the converts in New York State.

They were much scattered, a family here and there, residing on their own homesteads, very many of them well-to-do farmers, and others struggling with poverty, finding it an almost impossible thing to make both ends meet; then, again, in many families of husband, wife and children there was not always that unanimity of feeling towards the new religion between the different members of the family that was desirable for happiness, from the fact that some were Believers, others not, and still others bitter opposers.

This state of affairs, contrasted with the happy family of united Believers at Watervliet, soon began to show itself in a
desire, not only on the
part of the Elders of the
society, but by the scat-
tered f a m i l i e s themselves, for a closer com-
m u n i o n which would
bring a greater unity of
purpose and accomplish
results n o t otherwise
attainable.

Shaker Village, at Watervliet, N. Y.

Meanwhile, on the 4th of May, 1781, Mother Ann, Fathers William Lee, James Whittaker and Samuel Fitch, Sisters Mary Partington and Margaret Leeland, left Watervliet with the intention of making an extended visitation, covering the Believers in the States of Massachusetts and Connecticut, as well as those in New York. Traveling, at that period, a distance of several hundred miles across the country was a matter of no small moment to accomplish. In those days the lightning express was horseback, the accommodation train the stage coach, and the rapid transit through freight the lumber wagon and horse, while the oxen and cart made up the way freight, all running on the same road-bed—the mammoth turnpikes, built to make transportation easy between the large towns and cities.

Presumably for ease and comfort, and the better facility offered for reaching the outlying homes of some of the Believers, Mother Ann and her party adopted the "lightning express," toned down to the Shaker idea of propriety and moderation, commensurate with the weighty matter they had in hand. At any rate, they started out in a southerly direction, and were not long on their journey before they arrived at the house of one of the faithful, one Benjamin Osborn, whose residence was on Tuckernot Mountain (now Mt. Washington,) Berkshire county, Mass. Here they were received with open arms, and tarried for the space of ten days, preaching to a large congregation of people on the Sabbath, who came in from the surrounding country to hear of the strange religion and to see the wonderful Mother Ann whose fame had

---

The first of our illustrations here given, is that of the first church built in the town of New Lebanon, N. Y., in the year 1785, by Father James Whittaker. The other, that of the present Church Family in the little village of Watervliet, once Niskeyuna, the first settlement and the birth place of modern Shakerism in America.

gone out before her.   On this occasion many converts were gathered into the fold.

Continuing their journey, almost in a due easterly direction, they came in time to the town of Enfield, Conn., where they visited David Meacham, another convert to Shakerism.   With him they remained about a week, preaching and teaching their peculiar doctrine.   Here they were threatened with violence by the ungodly, but still were allowed to pass out of town on their mission unmolested.

From Enfield they went in a northeasterly direction, passing again into the State of Massachusetts, to the town of Grafton, near Worcester, where they halted for three or four days at the house of John Maynard, after which they passed on eight miles further to the house of Daniel Wood, in Upton, who was a brother of Margaret Leeland, one of the visiting party.   Daniel had previously embraced the faith and was publicly preaching the Shaker religion.   With him they remained over the Sabbath, when they went on to the town of Harvard, visiting the house of Zaccheus Stevens, and, a few days later that of Isaac Willard, and from there to the "Square House," which they made their headquarters for nearly two years.

From here, in 1791, Mother Ann and the Elders visited the town of Petersham.   At this place they met with much harsh treatment, and were subjected to more abuse, Mother Ann subsequently said, than she ever received at the hands of any people.   During the following year they visited Shirley, Woburn, Lexington, and several other places, and in the month of November of the same year went to Ashfield, returning to Harvard the following May, 1783.   On the 4th of July of this year, Mother Ann and her party began their return trip to Watervliet, passing again through the town of Petersham, where, on the previous occasion they were given over to the hands of a mob, but now were received with respect.   Again they visited Enfield, Conn., and from there passed northward, halting at the towns of Stockbridge and Stephentown, Mass., then over the line into the State of New York, tarrying for a time in the town of New Lebanon, and arriving in Watervliet, after an absence of two years and four months, on the 4th of September, having occupied two months to a day on their journey homeward.

On this visitation they sowed the seed which took deep root and became the foundation of the first, and for many years thereafter the only communistic society in America.

But the great importance of gathering the faithful into a more united and harmonious condition, both in temporal and spiritual things, pressed heavily upon Mother Ann and the Elders, and became the subject of much prayerful consideration.   Upon one occasion Mother Ann imparted to the Believers a vision in which she saw them all advancing, but as a scattered people, wanderers in a strange land; suddenly they were encountered by a mighty wall which none could scale, and none could penetrate. Here they gathered, forming a mighty body, united with one mind and one purpose, when, before their astonished gaze, a glimmer of light appeared, displaying an opening in the wall before them to which they had been previously blind, but now through which they all could pass onward to the goal of success. This vision Ann interpreted as emblematical of the state of the scattered Believers, distant from each other, without the means of guidance or protection, and still farther encumbered by the fact that the foes of a man are of his own household. From this vision Ann predicted a gathering of the church, but was quick to add, "This will not be my work, but Joseph Meacham's with others—they will perform it." From this time forth, the Believers labored towards uniting their domestic interests in one common whole, so that the poor, with the rich, might share equally in the blessings of this life.

At this stage in the progress of the Society, Father William Lee, Mother Ann's brother, passed away in death, on the 21st of July, 1784, at the age of 44 yrs. His death seriously affected the Society, and was a sad blow to Mother Ann, to whom he had been a right arm of support. But it was soon to be called to meet a still heavier trial in the loss of its beloved founder, who followed in the footsteps of her much lamented brother, on the 8th of the following September, in the 49th year of her age. Her bodily remains lie interred in the little church cemetery of the Society at Watervliet, simply marked by a plain marble slab bearing this inscription : "Mo. Ann Lee, born Manchester, England, February 29th, 1736. Departed this life Septr. 8th 1784."

Upon the death of Mother Ann, Father James Whittaker succeeded to the leadership of the Society, and, as preliminary to the gathering in of the Believers, he ordered, in the year 1785, that a house of public worship be built at New Lebanon, which was speedily accomplished, and on the 29th of January, 1786, was occupied and dedicated to the service of God.

CHAPTER V.

FATHER JAMES WHITTAKER—ELDER JOHN HOCKNELL—ELDER JOSEPH MEACHAM.

FATHER JAMES WHITTAKER, who, upon the death of Mother Ann Lee, on the 8th of Sept. 1784, succeeded to the leadership of the Society of Shakers, was a man of uncommon ability. He was born in Oldham, near Manchester, England, February 28th 1751. His parents were members of the Quaker congregation of James and Jane Wardley, and of that number who afterwards embraced the Shaker faith. His father, Jonathan Whittaker, was more than anxious to accompany Mother Ann and her party to America, but the state of his health would not permit of it, and he was one of those who were reluctantly left behind, but who also remained steadfast in the Shaker faith to the end.

James Whittaker's mother's maiden name was also Ann Lee, and probably a distant relation of Mother Ann, although the relationship, if any, has not been made apparent in any of the Shaker literature. She probably died while James was a youth, for we find him placed at an early age under the care of Mother Ann. As a child, he evinced a religious tendency far beyond his years. His testimony in after life, that though in childhood brought up as he was by Mother Ann in the way of God, he knew no guile, still felt himself a child of wrath, and cried most mightily to God for salvation, is indicative of that trait of character found as a most prominent feature in all the individuals who were the founders of Shakerism, and who are of that order to-day. They were then, as now, men and women endowed with an extremely emotional nature, and as ardently believed in the female Christ in Ann Lee as in the male Christ in Jesus. And to-day the advocates of woman's rights can nowhere find stronger defenders of the doctrine of perfect equality of men and women than among the Shakers. It is the very foundation stone of their religion, and upon which they have built their superstructure of Communism which has proved such a remarkable success.

James Whittaker always had been a constant companion and a right arm of defense to Mother Ann. From the time of her incarceration in the Manchester jail, when as a lad he conveyed food to her, through the key-hole of her cell door to save her from starvation, up to the hour of her departure into the land of spirits from her home in Niskeyuna, he never once disappointed her by wavering in the faith; and to him, perhaps, more than to any other one of her followers, did she look as the agent through which the Shaker doctrine and church would be made complete after her demise.

It was a most critical hour for Shakerism. It required men and women of ability and superior business qualifications to formulate a church covenant and order of Communism that would be acceptable to the Shaker rich in this world's goods, as well as to the poor and needy who were to profit by the change.

That feature of Christianity—equality of wealth—which it was sought to establish as the doctrine of Christ, was not held in favor by the wealthy of the world's people. They most strenuously opposed any idea of a reduction in their ranks, or to the right claimed by individuals to donate their entire property to such a "religious craze as Shakerism," which they declared to be "works of the devil," and prosecuted by leaders with selfish motives and profligate natures, who would spend in luxurious living all the property within their control, and then leave their victims to be supported by the community of which they had previously been well-to-do members. Then, again, the Shaker idea of celibacy was the rankest kind of immorality in their eyes, and it was not to be tolerated. "It was a coat of the thinnest material which covered the foulest type of licentiousness," they said, "and if permitted to exist, would result in a second Sodom and Gomorrah."

Almost the entire world's people were united to a man in the desire to stamp out the new and strange doctrine of Shakerism at any cost, and they hailed with delight the news of the death of Mother Ann, which they regarded as an interposition of Divine Providence in thus cutting her off at the early age of forty-eight, and which must result in the complete overthrow of the "devilish doctrine" that was ensnaring so very many worthy members of the regularly established churches, and others in the community. So, with her death they soon expected to see a breaking up of the sect and a total annihilation of the religion that had gained, in spite of all their efforts to suppress it, such a foot-hold in their midst. What, then, was their dismay when they beheld the measures taken to establish Shakerism on a broader and more substantial basis under the leadership of James Whittaker.

This was also a time of trial of faith for the Believers. Hundreds of the new converts were hardly prepared to make the full and complete sacrifice of all their worldly possessions, which Shakerism demanded for the good of the multitude. Personal selfishness, that bane which ever stands in the way of Christian progress, stood as a menace in the pathway of many. But the leaders stood firm. "If thy hand offend thee, cut it off! If thy eye offend thee, pluck it out!" was their watchword. No one was to be rejected because of his poverty, and no one refused because of his riches; but, one and all, they must prove their sincerity by giving up the world and all its sensual enjoyments, by a complete sacrifice of every selfish feature of humanity of whatever name and nature it might partake. Thus did Father James and his associates mark out the ground-plan of their religion.

The first discourse delivered by Father James in their new house of worship, in 1786, was a powerful appeal to his hearers to obey the voice of the Lord that his blessing might rest upon them as the true people of God. It was early made manifest to the self-recognized Board of Elders that New Lebanon would be the central home of the first church, and from this point must come the Shaker covenant which should define true Shakerism and contain the law by which all Shakers must be governed.

To Elder John Hocknell, the oldest of all the Shakers, he who was noted far and near for his meek deportment and great generosity, much was due the success they had so far achieved. Indeed, it was from his liberal purse that Mother Ann and her associates were enabled to cross the ocean and establish themselves here in America. It was his generous hand which purchased the tract of land in the backwoods of Niskeyuna. It was from his bounty that the funds were supplied which built the first habitations that sheltered them from the inclemency of the weather, and provided for all their temporal wants. In years he outnumbered Mother Ann by more than half a score, and was the senior of Father James by eight and twenty years. It was his great liberality and zeal which sustained the society in its infancy; his honesty and uprightness which gave character to the order as they advanced; and, now, he was to crown the greatest work of his life by giving to God, through the medium of Shakerism his entire worldly possessions, making himself by this act a living example of noble unselfishness, which is the dominant characteristic of every Shaker. Elder John, as he was called, departed this life on the 27th of February, 1799, much lamented by all who knew him, but lived to see his magnanimous act a grand success.

Joseph Meacham, another most worthy member of the Shakers, and one of the first in America to accept of the new and strange religion, was a prominent Elder in the fraternity. Previous to his uniting with the Shakers, he was a minister in the Baptist denomination in his native town of Enfield, Conn., where he was distinguished for his private virtues and exemplary life. He was endowed with superior natural ability, with a sound, philosophical and practical turn of mind, and withal possessed a spiritual nature which well fitted him for a leader.

Nearly the whole talent of the church was concentrated at New Lebanon until about the middle of January, 1787, when by advice of the Elders, Father James prepared for an extended visitation into Connecticut and Massachusetts, to look after the interests of the Society in the various sections of those States where Shakerism had gained a foothold.

His first visit was to Enfield, Conn., where he tarried for a short time, passing from there to the Believers in Harvard, Shirley, Woburn and other places, returning to Enfield in the month of March of the same year. In the prosecution of his arduous labors, he contracted a severe cold, which terminated in his death on the 20th of July. in the thirty-seventh year of his age. Thus passed away another faithful minister of Christ, who brought the gospel of Shakerism to this land. His death was keenly felt by every Shaker.

Father James was succeeded in the Ministry by Elder Joseph Meacham, who ever after was known as Father Joseph, and considered by the Believers as having a gift of Divine revelation deeper than that of any other preceding Shaker, with the exception of Mother Ann. To him are ascribed many of the peculiar devotional exercises originating from the spirit world under whose guidance he, also laid the foundation of the temporal economy of the Shakers. He was unhesitatingly received by every Shaker as the authoritative means of communication through whom Mother Ann and the other spirits of departed Shakers, and even Christ himself, made known to those on earth who remained steadfast in the faith, the way of salvation. His was the master-hand in all of the spiritual manifestations which occurred in New Lebanon and vicinity sixty years and more before the name of the Fox sisters was heard in connection with modern Spiritualism in Rochester, and the events which characterized their performances as wonderful, hardly approached, in the slightest degree, the spirit manifestations of Father Joseph, the Shaker, and his associates.

CHAPTER VI.

JOSEPH MEACHAM AS LEADER—VISIT OF GEN. LAFAYETTE.

PREVIOUS to the succession of Father Joseph Meacham to the leadership of the Shakers, in 1787, there had been no regular organization of the fraternity. From the very outset, Mother Ann had been recognized by them as the divinely-inspired leader and originator of Shakerism, inasmuch as by her the second coming of Christ had been accomplished and made manifest to a suffering world. Therefore her word was regarded by every Believer as the law. She designated, as Ministers and Elders, those of the most spiritually-minded and nearest to her as associates in her great work. The order itself had become to be known as a Ministry. Naturally, Mother Ann appointed her apostles as did Christ his, and named her successor in the leadership, and they regarded him as possessed of the office by divine authority, which he assumed. They also recognized that her successor was empowered with all the rights and privileges so reverently accorded to Mother Ann, and from that day to the present time this administration of parental authority has been perpetuated.

The great importance of gathering in the converts into a closer relationship with the fountain-head, had been felt sometime before the death of Mother Ann, and after her death Father James sought to bring this union about by casting out all sin and selfishness and preparing the way for the change which must come. But the administrative genius of the Believers was Father Joseph Meacham. Upon his succession to the leadership, on the death of Father James, his head and hand made rapid progress in that direction. His wonderful ability for organization was displayed by establishing Shakerism on a most enduring basis. During his potential' career, he formulated a plan of gathering the Shakers into a body religious, not a body politic, or a body corporate, because it would be inconsistent with the character of the institution to be styled as of a secular nature. Their real and personal estate could not be treated as a joint tenancy, nor a tenancy in common, therefore it was made a *consecration—a consecrated whole.*

Again, officers of corporate bodies must be chosen or elected by a vote of the members thereof; their term of office limited by law; their powers and duties defined by law. Not so with Shakerism, they did not receive the forms or principles of their institution from civil and political governments, but from what they regard as Divine authority. Therefore "the Shaker Society, as such, can never connect itself with the world; from this it must ever remain in isolation."* They "do not and can not hold property as a community estate, whether real or personal. The property held in trust by them is all consecrated to God, and religious and charitable purposes."† Shakers do "ask governmental protection in the arrangement of a perpetuity and entailment of real and personal estate to the Shaker covenantal consecration and institution, on the ground that the whole estate is a consecrated possession, sacred alone to religious and charitable purposes, judged of by the religious constitution of Christianity as understood by the true followers of Christ."‡

"With one accord the people gathered to the new home. They came out from the relations of the world, sold their possessions, dedicated their souls to God, and gave up all they possessed to the gospel work. No higher incentive could inspire the minds of men. In this they were laying down their lives for their friends, and yet the foundation remains sure." In what follows of these editorial remarks which are found in the MANIFESTO for October, 1889, the Editor hits the nail squarely on the head when he says: "Those of the present day who build, must stand on the same foundation and build with material equally as pure in the sight of God, and in the same spirit of consecration, if they think to acquire a corresponding success in this world. An amalgamation of the two orders can never work satisfactorily. 'No man can serve two masters.' The old inheritance with its mutual associations, the customs and practices of the children of this world, can not otherwise than result in a failure, to an individual, to a family, or to a community."

Those who are deceiving themselves with the idea that society is to be transformed into a governmental, political communism which is to bring peace, contentment and joy to a suffering humanity, will do well to ponder on these words of wisdom.

As illustrative of the consecrations made by the Believers, the following is the contents of a quaint document bearing the signature of Peter Ayers, and executed by him in his own handwriting on the 10th of May, 1787:

"One horse, one wagon, one lot of tackling, two cows, one two-year old heifer, 27 sheep, 25 pounds of wool, one chaise, 60 pounds of flax, 130 pounds of tobacco; one axe, one saddle, one sleigh, one padlock, one pound worth of pork, 14 bushels of potatoes, one bed and bedding, 65 bushels of wheat, 16 bushels of rye, 4 bushels of corn, 2 sickles, 4 turkeys, 11 hens, one pair of plough irons, 2 chains, four dollars worth of fur, and 16 dollars in money." Closing with these words: "The above-mentioned account is what I brought with me when I came to the church."§

Peter was of German descent, and as a volunteer had entered the army in the struggle for Independence, and was present on the surrender of General Burgoyne at Bemus Heights, October 16, 1777. He was but nineteen years of age when he first heard of Mother Ann and the Elders, and it was in the month of May, 1780, that he concluded to make a visit to Niskeyuna and

---

* Shaker MANIFESTO for December, 1882, p. 266. †*Ibid.* ‡*Ibid.*
§ Shaker MANIFESTO for October, 1882, p. 219.

learn for himself what this new and strange religion meant.   He said his visit was largely one of curiosity, as he understood that they were a peculiar and much deluded people.   Not feeling quite sure about the potency of the vagaries and enchantments which might beset him before his return, he decided to supply himself with home-made food, in order to guard against any spell that might result from partaking of the hospitality of the Shakers, should it be offered him.   However, he arrived safely at his destination and found a cheerful welcome, and the first half day passed in a social intercourse on matters of common interest with several of the Brethren, so that the noon-hour arrived before Peter hardly realized that it was approaching. He received an invitation from Elder John Hocknell to dine with them, when he met with the remark from Mother Ann: "Nay, we will let our brother Peter eat the food which he has brought with him, as he prefers to do that rather than to dine with us."   Poor Peter! this was like a thunder-clap out of a clear sky.   How did Mother Ann know his thoughts? How did she find out what he had been so very careful to conceal? Verily, her powers of enchantment were about to enthrall him; but when Elder John said to him very solemnly: "Young man, you ought this day to confess your sins and live a new life!" supplemented by the words of Mother Ann: "Yea, but let Peter go home to his parents, and have time to labor in his mind, then he can come again," he was only too glad of the opportunity to make his escape.   However, when once well out from under the immediate influence of the spell, he found Mother Ann's words coming true, for he began "to labor in his mind," and to feel a desire to return for more light on a subject which began to interest him greatly.   Peter subsequently made several visitations to the Shakers, and a short time after embraced the faith, but continued to reside at home with his parents for nearly eight years, when he made his home at New Lebanon until 1792.   This year he went with Elder Job Bishop to Canterbury, N. H., to organize a society there, where he spent the remainder of his days, dying an honored member of the Shaker fraternity in 1857, at the good old age of ninety-seven years and two days.

Another instance of the peculiarity of Shakerism is found in an incident occurring to General Marquis de Lafayette.   Upon one occasion when in the service of Gen. Washington, on a mission to Albany to negotiate with the Indians to secure their aid against the British, hearing about the Shakers, he visited them at Niskeyuna.   In company with another officer in regimental dress he entered very quietly the building where one of their devotional meetings was in progress.   The one among the brethren most eccentrically exercised, was Abijah Worster.   His outward manifestations were of a very curious type.   He was under a spell of singular, violent agitations; jerking, shaking, and suddenly twisting in convulsions in a most remarkable manner.   Lafayette's tall and manly form arose in the seat he occupied near the door, and he passed down directly to the front of the congregation and seated himself by Abijah's side and fastened his eyes upon him most intently, and as Abijah felt moved upon by the spirits to go into convulsions, Lafayette would reach out his arm and lay his hand upon the subject under agitation. This disconcerted Abijah not a little, and he began to feel the presence of the distinguished visitor with some alarm. Finally, with much effort, he gasped, "You seem desirous of obtaining this power." But the reply he received, in a calm, clear voice, "It is desirable,". so worked upon Abijah, that he suddenly arose and ran out of the door, followed as suddenly by the General who kept close by his side. To break the connection, Abijah hurried to the barn, but with his silent investigator close upon his heels. To make a show that he had business there, Abijah seized a broom and commenced a most vigorous sweeping of the floor, but there stood his inquisitorial friend waiting patiently to see what the next move would be. Abijah, in dismay, started for the house; as quickly in his footsteps was he who stuck to him closer than a brother. Almost vanquished, Abijah lifted the hatchway and rushed into the cellar; but lo! Lafayette was there also. In great confusion, Abijah rallied for one more effort, and grasping a rude ladder started to ascend to the floor above, but close upon the rounds was the unrelenting Lafayette, with a determination to learn what power or impulse controlled the man who was possessed with such strange actions. The opening in the floor led to the room in which were assembled Mother Ann and the Elders. Then, for the first time, Lafayette found voice enough to eagerly ask of them what manner of man he had encountered, and what was the nature of his malady? He was informed that it was wholly of a religious type, and that such dwelt among them. The tenet of their religion was then explained to him, when he inquired to know why he could not share in it as well as others; but Mother Ann informed him that his mission was of the world, and on the great earth plane before him; that in the soldier-life which he had chosen, he had a work to do of vast importance, as in the success of the patriotic arms that of the freedom of the populace depended.

CHAPTER VII.

SHAKER PUBLICATIONS—THE NINE CARDINAL VIRTUES OF SHAKERISM—COVENANT—WOMAN'S RIGHTS.

THE doctrine of Shakerism, as expounded by Father Joseph Meacham, and upon which he founded the organization of that Communal Society in New Lebanon, in 1787, is set forth in a work entitled "Christ's Second Appearing," by the United Society of Shakers, the first edition of which was published in 1808, at Lebanon, Warren County, Ohio. This was the first publication ever made by the society, and the only authentic work setting forth the tenets of their religion.   The only other publications previous to this, which had in a measure received the approbation of the Shakers, were "A Concise Statement of the Principles of the only true Church," which was but a small pamphlet, written by special request to a deaf man, and printed at Bennington, Vt., in the year 1790; and a pamphlet published in 1797, bearing the title of "The Kentucky Revival."

A revised edition of "Christ's Second Appearing" was published at Albany, N. Y., in 1810; also a third edition, in Cincinnati, Ohio, in the year 1823; and still a fourth edition, in Albany, N. Y., in 1854.

A copy of the book was sent to Thomas Jefferson, who afterwards informed the Shakers, for whom he had great respect: "I have read it through three times, and I pronounce it the best church history that was ever written, and if its exegesis of Christian principles is maintained and sustained by a practical life, it is destined, eventually, to overthrow all other religions."

The argument advanced as convincing proof of the correctness of the Shaker position on theology is too lengthy to be incorporated in this paper; besides, our investigations must be confined to the line of the historical and communistic feature of the order.   Therefore, to all who may desire a full and complete knowledge of Shakerism, we advise a reading of "Christ's Second Appearing," which quite likely may be found in most of the public libraries; if not, it can be procured by communicating with any of the Shaker societies.

Great difficulty will be found in the attempt to separate the civil from the religious feature in Shakerism, for they go hand in hand, and are inseparable; indeed, were it not for the religious element, the communistic feature would prove a failure, as have all other attempts in this direction which have neglected to eliminate selfishness, root and branch, and which has proved to be the great stumbling-stone in the pathway of success.

The nine cardinal virtues of Shakerism are:

1st. Purity in mind and body—a virgin life.

2d. Honesty and integrity of purpose in all words and transactions.

3d. Humanity and kindness to both friend and foe.

4th. Diligence in business, thus serving the Lord.   Labor for all, according to strength and ability, genius and circumstances.   Industrious, yet not slavish; that all may be busy, peaceable and happy.

5th. Prudence and economy, temperance and frugality, without parsimony.

6th. Absolute freedom from debt, owing no man anything but love and good-will.

7th. Education of children in scriptural, secular, and scientific knowledge.

8th. A united interest in all things—more comprehensive than the selfish relations of husband, wife, and children—the mutual love and unity of kindred spirits, the greatest and best demonstration of practical love.

9th. Ample provision for all in health, sickness and old age; a perfect equality—one household, one faith, practicing every virtue, shunning all vice."

With this as the fundamental ground-work of Shakerism, the converts who sought to join the order were required, as an evidence of their sincerity, to pay all of their just debts, and to discharge all legal obligations resting upon them, and, as far as possible, to make restitution for all the wrong committed by themselves against any of their fellow-creatures.

Under Father Joseph Meacham, the Shaker Society was divided into different orders, or classes. The first, or non-communal class, were those who received faith and came into a degree of relation with the Society, but chose to live in their own families and manage their own temporal concerns. They were to be regarded as Brethren and Sisters in the gospel, so long as they lived up to its requirements. Members of this class were not to be controlled by the Society, with regard to either their property, families or children. They could act as freely in all of these respects as did the members of any other religious society. Such persons were admitted to all the privileges of religious worship and spiritual communion belonging to this order, and also received instruction and counsel, according to their needs, whenever they expressed a desire for it, not being debarred from any privilege, by reason of their location, so far as circumstances would admit; and they might retain their union with the Society provided they did not violate the faith and the moral and religious principles of the institution. They were, however, requested always to bear in mind the necessity and importance of a spiritual increase, which would ultimately bring them within the fold of the Church Family—the highest in the order of Shakerism—and without which they would ever be exposed to the temptation of falling back again into the world.

The communal body of Shakers, or Shakerism proper, was divided into three classes, called Families. The first, or Novitiate Family, located at a little distance from the Church Family, and composed of all the probationary members, being under the special care, direction and instruction of four of the Elders of the Church Family, two of each sex, called Novitiate Elders. Here the novitiate was fitted and prepared for advancement in Shakerism at the will of the candidate, or they were at full liberty to return to the world, if, after a full understanding of the requirements of the order, they did not find themselves in full sympathy therewith.

If the candidate was bound by the ties of matrimony to an unbelieving partner, he was refused admission, unless a separation was the mutual desire of both husband and wife, or a legal separation accomplished under the civil laws of the land. And under such circumstances, if the convert was the husband, he must, before admission would be granted, convey to his wife, a just share of all his possessions.

The following is the Novitiate Covenant which all were then, as they are now, required to sign who present themselves as candidates for this order :—

Whereas; I, the undersigned, have this day attached myself as probationary member to the United Society of Believers at——, and it being my desire to live with said Society according to the known faith and customs thereof, that I may receive the benefits arising from the observance of the rules, regulations, moral, and relig ious instructions of the same: *Therefore,* agreeably to the custom of said Society, I hereby covenant, promise and agree, that I will never prefer any account, claim nor demand against the said Society, or any member or members thereof, for the USE of any money or property brought into said Society, nor for any labor or service which I may perform or render while residing in the same, over and above what I may receive in food, clothing, washing and other necessary support: And, whereas, it is further mutually understood and agreed that I shall be free to withdraw from said Society whenever I am dissatisfied therewith, and that after sufficient and timely notice shall have been given by me I shall receive all the money and other property which I brought into said Society, or their value at the time it was brought in: *Therefore,* I further agree and promise that so long as I am permitted to enjoy the benefits and privileges of said Society I will faithfully conform to the rules thereof, and will not find fault with the said rules, requirements, regulations, worship nor teachings, by acting or speaking against the same so as to create dissatisfaction, disunion, or inharmony in the family; provided this shall not be so construed as to prevent a free and respectful inquiry of the leading authority into the reasons of said rules and regulations; and if I shall fail to comply with this agreement such failure shall be deemed sufficient cause for loss of membership with said Society, and upon being desired so to do by the leading authority of the family in which I reside, will peaceably withdraw from the same.

Witness my hand the —— day of —— A. D. 18

(Signed.)

Attest.

The second, or Junior Family, is composed of those who have come into the order under the same covenant as the Novitiate, but untrammeled by the embarrassments of those of the matrimonial class and are thus enabled to devote themselves more freely to the furtherance of spirituality in their own lives, and, in consequence, receive greater enjoyment which comes from the feeling that they are one step. further advanced toward perfect Shakerism. In this order, as well as in the Novitiate, all are amply provided for in health, sickness and old age ; also, they may retain the lawful ownership of all their property as long as they may desire ; or they may donate the use of any part, or all, of their property for the mutual benefit of the family with which they are connected, and the property itself may be resumed at any time ; or they may dedicate a part, or the whole, and consecrate it forever to the support of the institution.

The third, or Senior Family, denominated as the Church, is composed of all those who have had sufficient time and opportunity to practically prove the faith of Shakerism, and are prepared to enter freely, fully and voluntarily into a united and consecrated interest. These covenant and agree to devote themselves and all they possess to the service of God and the support of the gospel, forever; solemnly promising never to bring debt or damage, claim or demand, against the Society, or any member thereof, for any property or service they may have devoted to the use and purpose of the institution. And to the credit of Shakerism, it can be truthfully said that during a period of more than one hundred years, since the permanent establishment of the Society at New Lebanon, there has never been a legal claim entered by any person for the recovery of property brought into the Society, neither has any person, peaceably withdrawing, ever been sent away empty-handed.

To enter this order of perfect Christianity is the aim and end of every true convert to Shakerism; and it is claimed to be by those who are participants in its blessings, as the Millennium—the thousand years reign on earth of the saints. They "testify that this manner of life is as much superior to the life of the world, as the heavenly is above the earthly; that they can not portray the inner feelings of joy and soul satisfaction of an approving conscience, and a life untarnished with fleshly lusts; that the great uprising of woman's claims in this day are all converging to this life of virgin purity, where all the higher demands of her being will be satisfied in Shaker organizations of Christian communism; that they who feel called to live after the manner of the angels, in heaven, neither marry nor are given in marriage; ask that those who have been led to believe that they are following Jesus, and living Christian lives in the practice of those things in which he never engaged, should now see their mistakes, turn from the error of their ways, and through repentance and tribulation of soul, enter into the work of regeneration."*

From the pages of the "Shaker Compendium" we glean the following:—

The members of the Church Family are all entitled to equal benefits and privileges, and no difference is ever made on account of the property any individual may have contributed.

Well defined, fixed principles which are perfectly understood and cordially received by all of the members, constitute the foundation of the Shaker government.

The rulers are but the executive of these principles, and the laws deduced therefrom; and they seek to bring the principles, so approved, to bear upon the consciences and affections of the ruled. And it is to accomplish this end that the male and female elements are equally balanced in the government; the former appealing more especially to the rational faculty in human nature; the latter to the affectional.

The Ministry is the central executive of the whole order, and consists of

---

* "Plain Talks concerning the Shakers," page 23.

two Brethren and two Sisters; and, in addition to this, every regularly organized family in a Society, has two Elder Brethren and two Elder Sisters, who have charge of the spiritual affairs; also two deacons and two deaconesses, who have the care of the temporal business; all other positions of care and trust are filled after the same dual order.

The utmost deference and respect is shown the opposite sex, in every department of the order, and this is a characteristic of the Shaker Brethren. Therefore, here, if nowhere else, the most zealous advocate of "woman's rights" should find the practical solution of the problem of the equality of the sexes.

The Shaker deems it marvelously inconsistent for any human government to be administered for the sole benefit of the political party in power; or that more than one half of the citizens should be disfranchised because they happen to be women, and compelled to obey laws they never sanctioned, and often in which they have no faith, and obliged to submit to taxation in which they have had no voice; but that the climax of inconsistency is reached when Brethren and Sisters, members of the same religious body, are divided into the rich and poor in the things of this temporal world, but who are vainly expecting that in the world to come, they shall be willing to have eternal things in common.

Communal organizations have been the one thing sought, for many ages, and many have been the attempts to establish them on both civil and religious grounds, and apparently under the most favorable circumstances, yet they have as often failed; but the cause of such failure is not hidden, and the promoters of all communal associations will do well to take a lesson in Shakerism before making an attempt to establish any communistic society composed of unregenerate humanity.

The Shakers teach that Shakerism, instead of attending solely to the spiritual necessities of man for only one day in seven, cares for and supplies all his temporal, as well as spiritual wants, all the seven days of the week.

CHAPTER VIII.

MOUNT LEBANON COMMUNITY—MINISTRY ESTABLISHED—BUSINESS OPERATIONS.

FIRST in the order of the established Communities of Shakerism was that of the New Lebanon Society. This was located in the town of New Lebanon, N. Y., near the Massachusetts state line on the west side of the Berkshire Hills, and on the eastern edge of the town of New Lebanon.

In 1861 this Shaker settlement was so flourishing as to warrant the Brethren

MOUNT LEBANON, NORTH FAMILY, N. Y.

MOUNT LEBANON, N. Y.—THE CHURCH FAMILY.

in asking the general government to make it a post-office station. This was granted on the 17th of August in that year, and the Postmaster-General, Montgomery Blair, appointed a very worthy Shaker, Elder Richard Bushnell, as the postmaster, designating the new office as Mount Lebanon, in order to distinguish it from the older office of New Lebanon located in another part of the town. From this time the Society became to be known as the Mount Lebanon Shakers, and this name it has ever since retained, and hereafter in speaking of it we will so designate it.

In the month of September, 1787, Father Joseph Meacham, Elders Calvin Harlow and David Meacham, notified all those who had accepted the Shaker faith that the time was ripe for the formation of a church organization, and that all who desired, and were qualified, might come into the association. Only those who were sound in the faith, free from debt, independent of all obligations to others, and single persons, were to be admitted. Generally this included adults, but in some exceptional cases, children who had the free and full consent of their parents, were admitted.

This collective body of Christians, voluntarily withdrawing themselves from the world and all its attachments, formed what was to be known as the first church of the United Society of Believers—the Church Family of Shakerism. However, to provide for many who had accepted of a degree of the Shaker religion but were still bound by family ties, and for others who were seekers after the truth and on probation, a "family relation order," distinct from the Church was established, into which this class were gathered to be properly educated for the higher plane of Shakerism. Within the Church was established a Ministry, which constituted the authority and fountain-head of all Shaker government. This consisted of two Brethren and two Sisters—Father Joseph Meacham, Abiatha Babbett, Mother Lucy Wright and Ruth Landon.

Before the close of the year 1787, the Church had a membership of more than one hundred persons, not including those in the Family and Novitiate Order. Provision for the support of the Community had been made by the generous donations of Hezekiah Hammond, Jonathan Walker, David Darrow, and others, of their homes and lands; still they were over crowded and sadly lacked for houses for their accommodation, and more land for farming purposes and buildings for the use and occupancy of the rapid accessions which were coming in from all quarters. But, under the wise management of Father Joseph, this was soon provided for, by his erection on the 27th of August, 1788, of the framework for an extensive dwelling for the accommodation of the Church. This structure was rapidly carried forward to completion, and was ready for occupancy on the following Christmas.

The Ministry appointed Elders as directors in the spiritual management in each of the established orders. Trustees were also delegated to take charge of the temporal affairs of the association, the buying and selling of all property, and as custodians of the deeds of the real estate purchased for the Society.

About the same time, the Society at Watervliet was also organized. True, in point of time, this was the oldest association of the Shakers, but the second in the order of organization into a body corporate. Two Families were established here, but both under the immediate jurisdiction of the Ministry at Mount Lebanon. The Watervliet and Mount Lebanon Societies formed what was denominated as a Bishopric. Elder John Hocknell resided at Watervliet, and was instrumental in the establishment of this Society, and donated his large landed estate for that purpose. The Ministry made the appointment, as Senior Elders over the Watervliet Society, of Timothy Hubbard and Anna Mathewson, and of Aaron Wood and Sarah Bennett as their associates.

The year 1788 was one bordering upon hardship for the infant Societies. The wheat crop, which had been regarded as the main source of supply for their food, was nearly ruined by the cold and open winter, and from the same cause the fruit crop was almost a total failure. But upon a just and equal division of the harvest being made to all the Families, though limited in quantity, there was no actual suffering for the want of food.

The next year, 1789, more attention was given to the raising of potatoes, which resulted in securing a harvest of some three thousand bushels as the outcome of their efforts. This, with a fair crop of wheat, rye, oats, barley, corn and flax was an evidence of thrift and proof of a determination on the part of the Shakers to make a success of their communistic Society.

In 1788, Elders Calvin Harlow and David Meacham went out on a visitation to the Shakers in the other States who were not as yet gathered into organized Societies. Five years later at least nine other Societies had been organized in the States of Connecticut, Massachusetts, New Hampshire and Maine, with a membership of upwards of one thousand souls.

In 1791, Elder David Meacham was appointed by the Ministry as the senior trustee and director of all business transactions with the general public. At the same time an order of deacons was established invested with the oversight of the temporal affairs of each family. The several orders of the Church were as follows: The Ministry, Elders, Trustees and family deacons. After this arrangement, the Ministry withdrew from the active management of all temporal duties to attend to that of the spiritual condition of the members, leaving the management of each of the other departments to its own delegated head, all being responsible, in all of their transactions, to their superiors. By-laws for the government of the Believers were committed to writing that all might understand and profit thereby. Some of the laws were to this effect: "No one shall buy or sell in the Church, nor trade with those outside of the Church, except by the union of the Trustees." "No one shall hold private property." "A selfish, private union should not be maintained, nor a private correspondence held with any person in or out of the Society."*

---

* "The MANIFESTO, 1889," page 194.

NEW DWELLING OF THE CHURCH FAMILY, with Meeting House adjoining, Mt. LEBANON, N. Y.

Church at Mount Lebanon, N. Y.

In 1793, a further addition to their landed estate was made by the purchase, at Mount Lebanon of several farms, but no debt was incurred by reason of any transaction. The Trustees were exceedingly careful in their business capacity and relations outside of the Society, where they were regarded as strictly honest and above reproach. The Brethren and Sisters who had in hand the management of the general business, held daily meetings for conference as to the best method to pursue, and each department moved on harmoniously.

In the line of manufacturing, that of tanning and currying was carried on by the community the very first year of its organization. The bark was ground by the old-style, upright, circular millstone, propelled by horse power. Several tan vats were sunk outside in the ground near the bark mill, and for twenty years this was the method pursued. In 1807, improvements were inaugurated by enlarging the building and putting in a machine for rolling sole-leather for boots and shoes. In 1813, they added a Richardson leather-splitting machine, which was then a new and patented invention for splitting leather. In fact, this was one of the first invented machines for that purpose. Still further improvements were made twenty years later by the enlargement of buildings and the putting down of more tan vats. But in 1850, the Shakers caught the spirit of the times, abandoned the olden-time cold liquor style, twelve months' process, of making good honest leather, and introduced the steam boiler, hot liquor vats and leaches, and forced along their stock in genuine "world's people" style, vastly more to the Shaker profit. But, a few years ago they concluded to abandon this branch of their business, probably arriving at this determination from a feeling that they could not consistently manufacture Shaker leather by the dishonest, high-pressure steam process.

The manufacture of wool hats was also one of their first occupations; and the making of cloth by the old hand-loom process was continued by them for many years. Saddle and harness making was also at one time a profitable department of their manufactures. In fact, we find nearly every trade well represented in their ranks—weavers, spinners, tailors, tanners, curriers, shoemakers, blacksmiths, machinists, masons, carpenters, tinsmiths; and in the line of the professions that of physicians. But we find them not burdened with saloons, and, consequently, without sheriffs, police or constables, lawyers, courts or jails.

The manufacture of medicines has been extensively carried on by the Mount Lebanon Society for many years. Shaker garden seeds have also a world-wide reputation. They are also extensive farmers and fruit growers. They have some three thousand acres of land besides several timber tracts in other parts of the country. They have a population of about three hundred at Mount Lebanon and one hundred and twenty-five at Watervliet. They are well supplied with buildings of substantial and superior character, and have ample accommodations for a thousand persons. The Society is looking for large accessions to its numbers at no distant day. They profess to read in the signs of the times a coming upheaval of society; that the present legalized system of granting power and advantage to the few at the expense of the many, is creating a discontent among the laboring class that can but result in the complete overthrow of the present system of society; but that before this will occur, the Shaker doctrine will spread over the land as an educator of the masses, teaching them that true and perfect happiness can only be enjoyed where every vestige of selfishness has been rooted out from the human heart, giving perfect equality to all and a community of goods such as is embraced in Shakerism.

CHAPTER IX.

MEN AND WOMEN ON EQUAL FOOTING—GATHERING OF COMMUNITIES IN OTHER LOCALITIES—ELDER JOHN WHITELEY.

IN the year 1793 the Church organization of Shakerism may be said to have been completed. The one important point of gospel order which they felt was indispensable to the true relation of the Church was perfected. Previous to this they had been held together by the kind and friendly relations which existed with them as with other religious bodies. But the promoters of Shakerism saw that something more was required if they were to be true followers of Christ and his teachings. They saw that the union of men and women for the worship of God one day in seven, leaving them to the machinations of the devil the other six days of the week, was not the true spirit of Christianity, therefore communism was established, in order that no man, woman or child within the order need lack for shelter, food or raiment; that the body, as well as the soul, might receive special care at their hands. To this end, the Brethren and Sisters, in their management of the general business, saw the necessity of often conferring with each other as to the best means and methods to be used in order to accomplish the best results. Meetings were held every other day, and sometimes oftener. As officers, the Sisters held equal privileges with the Brethren in all their conferences. Thus Shakerism accords to woman an equal voice with man in the government of the Society.

Before the house of worship at Mount Lebanon was built, the Shakers, as a body, had no regular order of religious service. Being scattered over a wide extent in small families, they spent their hours of worship mostly in their own homes. Where several of the families were located near each other, meetings would be held at some designated place, and a Minister, or one of the Elders, would direct the service. If, however, they were within a few

COMMUNITY AT ENFIELD, CONN.

hours' ride of Watervliet, they would consider it a privilege to make the journey in order to meet Mother Ann and the Elders and enjoy the short season of spiritual communion which their presence gave.   The inclemency of the weather was never such as to induce them to remain in their more comfortable houses, and on many dark and stormy days they were noticed wending their way toward Watervliet.   Here they would assemble in one of the houses and hold their meetings.   At first, all would sit in silence, then some one of the assembly would begin the exercises by the singing of a solemn song, or one of the Elders would lead with an exhortation, to be followed with prayer ; or, perhaps, some brother or sister would be moved upon spiritually, which would be made manifest by convulsions of the body, shaking, twisting, turning and marching in the Shaker dance.

Community at Harvard, Mass.

After the building of the Mount Lebanon church, the exercises were of a more orderly nature—the marching and dancing were more moderate.   The violent manifestations of a spiritualistic nature became less frequent.   The meetings on Sunday, in the morning, were of a public nature, which the "world's people" if they chose, could attend.   For the benefit of the worshipers, small pegs were driven into the floor, to aid the Brethren and Sisters in the forming of straight ranks, as they stood to sing and to speak.   At the hour when the service was to begin, they assumed a standing position, and the Brethren and Sisters arranged themselves in ranks upon opposite sides of the house, the head of the columns being separated from each other by about four feet, while at the foot of the columns they were some ten feet apart.   Thus arranged, they were in readiness for their marching dance and the exercise known to them as the "Square Order."   This religious service, to which the public were admitted as silent spectators, was participated in by all the Shaker families, with the exception of that of the Church family, the highest in the order of Shakerism, they held their services in the afternoon of the Sabbath, to which none not of their rank were ever admitted. Of the ceremonies conducted within this hallowed precinct of their gatherings, we have no information. Their secrets have been held more sacred and have been better kept, than have those of the Masonic fraternity. No William Morgan among them has disregarded his solemn obligations to the order so far as to enlighten the Gentile mind in the mysteries of this sublime degree of Shakerism.

The first Shaker Hymn Book, published exclusively for the Shakers, was issued by themselves, at Hancock, Mass., in 1813, emanated from one of the families located there, and bore the title, "Millennial Praises." Among the "world's people," this book would hardly rank as a poetical effusion. It is rather a tirade against the sins of the flesh. Some very pointed and plain truths are told in language seeking to convey to the Shaker heart, unmistakable words, some particular sin to be ostracized, which fully expresses the ideas which inspired the founders of the order. We note some of the unique titles of the hymns: "Cause and Effect of Man's Fall," "Resolution against a Carnal Nature," "Make thy Garden Grow," "Natural and Spiritual Relation," and many others of like character in this book of two hundred and eighty-eight pages.

In the year 1790, a community of the Shakers was gathered in the town of Hancock, Mass., and in the month of September Elder Calvin Harlow was appointed to take charge of that Community. At the same time, Sister Sarah Harrison was appointed to the Ministry. The other officers were selected from the members of the Hancock Society. Thus was successfully launched another branch from the parent Society at Mount Lebanon, which has now already entered upon its second centennial year. In the following May, 1791, a community was gathered at Harvard, Mass., making the fourth Shaker Society in its order of establishment. The parent Society appointed Eleazer Rand and Hannah Kendall over this branch. In the month of February, 1792, another branch was established at Canterbury, N. H., under the guidance of Job Bishop and Hannah Goodrich. At the same time two other branches were established, one at Enfield, Conn., and the other in Shirley, Mass; that at Enfield, under Calvin Harlow and Sarah Harrison, and at Shirley under the ministerial guidance of Eleazer Rand and Hannah Kendall.

The Shaker Community at Shirley, Mass., originated by the donation of Elijah Wildes of his farm, and of others strong in the Shaker faith. They were especially strengthened in their early days by such solid and prominent members as Nathan Willard, Oliver Burt, Amos Buttrick and Ivery Wildes. The Society at Shirley was organized in the year 1793, with a membership of forty-four adults and twenty-two youths and children. From this humble beginning many hundreds here have found a home, some for a longer and some for a shorter period of time. The pretty, little, well-filled cemetery attests that a goodly number have held on to the end.

ELDER JOHN WHITELEY.

COMMUNITY AT SHIRLEY, MASS.

Extending their domains by purchase and other accessions, they now hold the ownership of some two thousand five hundred acres of land. Farming, the raising of garden seeds, the manufacture of Shaker brooms, dish and floor mops, with the celebrated Shaker apple sauce and some other articles, are their chief means of support.

John Whiteley, who came to America from England fifty years ago, is the presiding Elder and the business manager of this Society. A more upright and honorable man, and in whose countenance the index of his character is more plainly stamped, never walked the streets of Shirley. Elder Whiteley has also the general superintendency of the Society at Harvard, Mass. The business there chiefly carried on is farm and dairy work, and the preparation of medicinal herbs. They have also a large estate in acreage. The present number of able and devoted workers at both Shirley and Harvard is not large, but they are patiently watching and waiting.

Thus we have seven distinct settlements of communistic Societies of Shakerism, each one of which has now successfully passed into its second centennial year with a present membership of some one thousand souls, and as proprietors of about thirty thousand acres of land, with buildings unsurpassed for comfort and durability by any farming and manufacturing community in the land.

In the following February, 1793, another branch of the parent Society was gathered in the town of Alfred, Me., where John Barnes and Sarah Kendall were delegated as the presiding Elders. This settlement, shortly after, was followed by any other branch at Enfield, N. H., and about the same time other Societies were established, one in New Gloucester, Me., another in Groveland, N. Y., and still another at Tyringham, Mass. This comprised all of the Shaker settlements made previous to the year 1794, no others being founded till 1805. They were all founded within a period of five years—1787 to 1793.

At the beginning of the year 1780, the entire Community of Shakers numbered no more than nine persons, all of whom came over from England. Twenty-three years later, 1803, they numbered one thousand six hundred and thirty-two. Twenty-five years later, a thousand more members had been added to their census, and by the end of the year 1839, the entire membership of the Shaker Societies numbered five thousand persons.

The Society at Enfield, N. H., was established about the same date, of that of Shirley, Mass., 1793. They have a beautiful situation along the west shore of Mascoma Lake. They have a large estate, and are chiefly interested in farming and dairy pursuits. They have a good stock of full-blooded, registered Durham cows. At the Church Family they have one of the finest barns for stock to be found in that section. It is one hundred feet long by fifty feet wide, a cellar running under the entire building, the walls of which are laid with large blocks of granite. The first floor has its stalls for the cows, a reservoir of water and a cooking tank, and a room for the storage of the herdsmen's tools. The boiler room and root cellar are both entered from this floor. The second loft is used as a feeding floor, where the hay is easily passed to the cow stalls on the floor below. The third floor is the "drive-way." An abutment at both ends of the barn forms an easy passage for the loads of hay on this floor, where the teams are unloaded and the hay stored on either side of the barn, after which the teams are driven out of the opposite end into the fields beyond. The building has a gable roof, and is covered with slate brought from the State of Vermont. The building was erected in 1854.

In cold weather the cow stalls are warmed by steam, to a temperature of about sixty degrees, through a line of pipes running the entire length of their apartments. The warm room for the cows, the warm food with which they are fed, and the warm water given them to drink in cold weather, amply pays for all the outlay, in an increased supply of milk.

CHAPTER X.

"KENTUCKY REVIVAL"—PECULIAR FORMS OF WORSHIP—SHAKERS SENT ON FOOT A THOUSAND MILES TO INVESTIGATE—PERSE- TIONS—COMMUNITIES ESTABLISHED IN KENTUCKY AND OHIO.

FOR the next twelve years, following 1793, Shakerism made no very marked progress. A moderate growth in numbers from admissions of members into the already established Societies was all that could be claimed.

In the years 1800 and 1801, in the southwestern portion of the State of Kentucky a most remarkable religious fervor swept over that entire commu- nity, which shortly after paved the way for the established of Shakerism in that distant State. An interesting account of this "most extraordinary out-pouring of the spirit of God"—so styled by some church members, while others designated it as the "works of the devil"—is to be found in a little work of 142 pages, entitled; "The Kentucky Revival," written by an eye- witness of the proceedings, Richard M'Nemar, and published in Cincinnati, Ohio, in 1807. We learn from him that for several years previous to the outbreak, the state of religion in that portion of Kentucky was at a very low ebb in the dominant churches, which were composed of the Presbyterian, Baptist and Methodist persuasions, and that although these different sects professedly set out to establish and promote the peaceable religion of Jesus, their usual debates and controversies brought to life a hot spiritual warfare, and that such was the zeal of each for their distinguishing tenets and forms of worship, that they held aloof from any communion or fellowship whatever with each other—in fact, treating each other with every possible mark of

COMMUNITY AT ENFIELD, N. H.

hostility. This, then, was the spiritual state of the churches. Meanwhile Deism began to spread rapidly over the community, and very many embraced that faith. This condition of affairs continued for several years, and until the year 1800, when, from the banks of the Gasper and Red Rivers, in the counties of Logan and Christian, a ripple of commotion came over those troubled waters that struck consternation into the hearts of many a household.

Reports came of strong men shaking as a reed in the wind; of an intense throbbing of the heart, with violent weeping; of being thrown in the street, and by no visible power; with a swooning away until every appearance of life had departed, and they lay as in a trance. Children were seized with the same influence. In time, some recovered from the trance with a shout of joy, others cried out for mercy. The infliction rapidly overspread the whole country. It broke out in Knoxville, and there was an outburst of it in Nashville, Tenn. Camp meetings were held in very many places to accommodate the throngs that crowded to witness the mighty power that was shaking the populace to its very center.

One of the most remarkable of these meetings was begun on the 22nd of May, 1801, in the town of Cabin Creek, and continued without intermission for four days and three nights. The scene is said to have been "awful beyond description." Many, in attempting to flee from its influence, fell by the way, and so many were they that they were collected together and laid out, covering two squares of the floor of the meeting-house, in order to prevent their being trodden under foot by the multitude.

At another general camp meeting, convened in the town of Concord, in Bourbon county, some four thousand persons gathered and met with like experiences. On another occasion, at a general gathering of some twenty thousand people at Caneridge, in the same county, on the 6th of August, it is said that three thousand persons fell to the ground in the state of trance. Later on, these persons formed themselves into a body of worshipers called Schismatics, or separators from the established churches.

When we read of their peculiar forms of worship, of their exercises in rolling, jerks and barks, we stand aghast, and ask ourselves if this people had run mad.

In the "rolling" exercise, they doubled head and feet together; and rolled over and over like a wheel; or, stretching themselves prostrate, they turned swiftly over and over like a log. This was considered as debasing and mortifying the flesh. But still more demeaning were the "jerks." This exercise commonly began in the head, which would fly backward and forward, and from side to side, with a quick jolt; then, with a violent dash on the ground, they would bounce from place to place, like a foot ball; or they would hop about with head, limbs and body twitching and jolting in every direction. But the last possible grade of mortification culminated in the "barks." In this they were exercised to take the position of the dog, and move about upon all fours, growling and barking, snapping of teeth, having every appearance of a most vicious beast. These exercises were acknowledged, by the victims, as being brought upon them involuntarily, and in punishment for disobedience, or as a stimulus to incite them to perform some duty to which they were opposed. And as it was inflicted upon those of cultivated and polite breeding, equally with those of lower birth, it would seem to the observer as though the candidate was moved by some supernatural power.

In the course of time these strange proceedings were superseded by the voluntary dance, and we read that "brother Thompson, at the spring sacrament, at Turtle Creek, in 1804, was constrained, just at the close of the meeting, to go to dancing, and for an hour or more to dance around the stand, all the while repeating in a low tone of voice—'This is the Holy Ghost—glory!'"

Before the close of the year 1804, the Schismatics, or New Lights religionists, as they were often called, had organized themselves into regular Societies, covering the States of Kentucky, Tennessee, North Carolina, Ohio, Virginia and Western Pennsylvania, their meetings characterized by the same wild fervor of praying, shouting, jerking, barking, rolling, prophesying and singing, as when the news of the first outbreak came down from the banks of the Gasper and Red Rivers in Kentucky.

Their mode of prayer was of the most singular form. Each one stood alone and by himself; each one was for himself, and himself alone in his separate and individual petition to Almighty God, which formed one united whole, by the sound of which thereof, it was said, the doubting footsteps of some, who were in search of the meeting, were directed there for miles.

Another singular feature of their exercise was the shaking of hands, and at the same time of pledging themselves each to the other, by the most solemn and sacred of vows, that they would persevere to the end in their sin-killing work.

Their songs and hymns were unique, the following being a specimen of a couple of verses from "Part First" of one of the latter, though Mr. M'Nemar remarks that the hymn itself was not originally intended for publication:

"The twenty-first of the third month, in eighteen hundred one,
The word of God came unto me—that word which came to John:
'My gospel is preparing for this benighted land;
Go and proclaim the tidings my kingdom is at hand.'

"With prayer and exhortation they make the forest roar,
And such loud strains of shouting were never heard before.
The stupid antichristians were struck both blind and dumb,
With such loud supplications, 'Lord, let thy kingdom come!'"

The following is from "Part Second" of the same hymn:

"Five preachers formed a body in eighteen hundred three,
From antichrist's false systems, to set the people free;

His doctrine and his worship in pieces they did tear,
But ere the scene was ended these men became a snare.

"The word of God came unto them in eighteen hundred four:
'Your work is now completed; you are called to do no more.
My kingdom soon must enter, I cannot long delay;
And in your present order you're standing in my way.' "

This, then, was the religious state of the western country which came by post to the Shaker Society at Mount Lebanon, and determined them to send as missionaries to that then far-off land, John Meacham, Benjamin S. Youngs and Issachar Bates. This journey of more than a thousand miles was made by them on foot, and attended with many privations and hardships. It was begun on the first day of January, 1805, and they arrived in Kentucky about the first of March. It was their intention to visit the scenes of the great revival and see for themselves how much was the work of God and how much that of man.

Here the feature of spirit impressions came in as a factor. It was this which impelled the ambassadors to take their long journey on foot to carry the "true gospel" to the land of the great awakening. And it was this same spirit impression that had led the multitude of subjects to form great expectations of a miraculous display of Divine power in the coming summer of 1805, and which was expressed in the words of their hymn:

"Shout! Christians, shout! the Lord is come!
Prepare, prepare to make him room.
On earth he reigns; we feel him near;
The signs of glory now appear."

The ambassadors remained for a few days at Paint Lick, where they were very kindly received, and then passed on to Caneridge and spent a few days more with the subjects of the revival there, and then passed over into Ohio, and paid their first visit to Springfield. From thence they went to Turtle Creek, a place near Lebanon, which they reached on the 22d of March, tarrying over night at the house of one Malcham Worley, who was a man of independent fortune and liberal education, as well as a man of unspotted character, and one of the most prominent men in all that region.

Mr. M'Nemar tells us that Malcham was one of the violent subjects of the great revival, and one of the first to embrace the new religion brought to his door by the Shaker ambassadors; and he says, "I was at first staggered, from a deep-rooted prejudice that I had imbibed against some of his peculiar sentiments, but finally concluded that if Malcham had been more wild in his former exercises than the rest, he certainly needed salvation the more. But I was not a little surprised that these strange Brethren should come directly there, and he receive them with such cordiality, when I was well assured that no previous acquaintance had existed between them."

Within three or four weeks from the time that Malcham embraced the faith, some ten or twelve families had joined him, and within a very short time after, some thirty families more had embraced the Shaker doctrine.

But the same spirit of persecution which followed in the footsteps of Mother Ann, and, indeed, every Shaker who attempted to preach his peculiar doctrine to a new people, began to break out in a violent form. First in the field against them was one Elder John Thompson, a minister of the gospel at Springfield, who, though at a distance from Turtle Creek, where the ambassadors from Lebanon were making proselytes, wrote to the church at that place, under date of April 5, 1805, in which he expressed his opinion of the Shakers in these words: "It matters not to me who they are, who are the devil's tools, whether men or angels, good men or bad. In the strength of God I mean not to spare; I used lenity once to the devil, because he came in a good man—namely, Worley. But my God respects no man's person; I would that they were even cut off who trouble you. I mean in the name and strength of God to lift his rod of almighty truth against this viper." And in virtue of his words he hastened to the camp meeting at Turtle Creek, on the 27th of the month, and raised a sudden and passionate outcry against the Shaker intruders, asserting that the Holy Ghost had made him the overseer of the flock, and that these Shakers were false Christs, false prophets, wolves in sheep's clothing, creeping into houses and leading captive silly women and sillier men; and, still further seeking to incite the populace against them by exclaiming in a loud voice: "They are liars! they are liars! Down with them and their pernicious doctrine!"

With such an example as this set before the people by a professing Christian minister, is it any wonder that a layman boldly spat in the faces of John Meacham and Issachar Bates, crying aloud: "Let us make a great fire and burn these false prophets from the face of the earth."

But notwithstanding these persecutions, the Shakers "waxed strong," and soon were planted two Societies in Kentucky and four in Ohio, numbering some two thousand souls, being augmented by members coming in from other adjoining States.

There are four families of Shakers at Pleasant Hill, Ky., the dwelling of the Church Family being shown in the accompanying sketch.

DWELLING OF THE CHURCH FAMILY AT PLEASANT HILL, KY.

Elder, Harvey L. Eads.

CHAPTER XI.

BIOGRAPHY OF BISHOP H. L. EADS, SOUTH UNION, KENTUCKY.

THE SHAKER COMMUNITY at South Union, Ky., has about three thousand acres of land. That noted, venerable Shaker, the late Bishop Harvey L. Eads, was at the time of his death, February 13, 1892, at the ripe old age of eighty-four years and ten months, the managing head of this Shaker Community, having been appointed to this position in 1872. He was the oldest minister in the order. The following biographical sketch of him is from the history of Kentucky, published in 1886 :—

"Bishop H. L. Eads, of Logan County, was born in a log cabin, near South Union, Ky., April 28, 1807, and is a son of Samuel G. and Sallie (Robinson) Eads. He joined the Society of Shakers in his mother's arms; at its first gathering, on the 17th of November following was 'given up to the Lord' and placed in 'the children's order' before he was one year old. All he is, or has, the Shakers made him and gave him, after obtaining his existence. He continued to live in a little log cabin until he was fifteen years old. After four years of age he attended school three months each year, learned to read, spell, write 'and 'tis said could cipher too' as far as the rule of three and vulgar fractions. All else (and he is the best read scholar, writer and logician ever reared among the Shakers) he has 'picked up' at spare moments. After he was six or eight years of age he worked sedulously at some manual labor for nine months each year; learned the shoemaker's trade by four years' active service; was a teamster for two years; a seed grower for eight years; was next elevated to the Ministry (1836) with Elder Benjamin S. Youngs, (the first missionary sent from the mother Society in New York to the West) and now 'paid his way' by learning and working at the tailoring and bookbinding trades. In 1844 he was suddenly called to Ohio; was then informed of his releasement from the capacity of a Bishop, and requested to make his home at the Union Village Society. This he did without inquiring the reasons for his displacement, and to this day he is ignorant of the cause. In Ohio he learned and worked two years at wool carding and spinning, also at the tin and sheet-iron works. He was appointed Novitiate Elder at Union Village, Ohio, in 1846, remaining at the same twelve years; there learned the printing, dentistry, painting and hat trades; was relieved of the Eldership in 1858, and worked as a common laborer for two full years, when he was again appointed the Elder of a senior family. At this as well as at the novitiate family he was very successful in his undertakings. At the opening of the civil war he was sent back to Kentucky to assume the position he so suddenly vacated in 1844—the junior bishop in the Society having been absent more than eighteen years ; next became one of the bishops in the consolidated Ministry of the two Kentucky Societies. In 1872 this consolidation was dissolved, and he became and has remained acting head of the Shaker Society at South Union, Ky."

Louis Basting, a member of the Shaker Society at West Pittsfield, Mass., in a recent communication.to the New York *Sun*, thus speaks of Elder Eads : "The death of Elder H. L. Eads, the head of the Shaker Community at South Union, Ky., removes a striking figure from the scene of action. The unique experience of having been born among Shakers was his, for his parents, shortly after marriage, were converted and united with the Society where he lived and labored during the eighty-five years of his life. He grew up among the very trying scenes of hardship and danger which marked the founding of the western Communities. His great natural abilities and evident devotion to the religious principles of the order soon caused him to be called to positions of trust and responsibility. The very limited education he received was of the most rudimentary quality, but the impulse for information being strong within him, he availed himself of every opportunity to enlarge his stock of knowledge, and by close application to study, when not engaged in manual labor or official duties, he became a talented public speaker, capable of meeting the arguments of every form of belief or unbelief. The works of Plato, Spinoza, and Locke were quite familiar to him, and gave to his discourses a logical turn and acute discernment, making them weighty and effective. His published criticisms of the infidel positions assumed by Tyndall and Ingersoll, and of the extreme orthodoxy of McCosh and Talmage, reveal not only great intellectual ability, but also the perfect fairness with which he met those of different belief and opinion."

"The outbreak of the civil war placed the Believers of Kentucky in a very difficult position. They had never owned slaves, and did not approve the institution which permitted it, and on that account were regarded with distrust and suspicion by the pro-slavery element of the neighborhood, while their peace principles, which forbade them to take up arms in defence of the Union, brought them into conflict with the authorities at Washington ; so that much tact was required on the part of the leaders to steer safely through those troublous times. Their settlements were often occupied by Northern and Southern forces, and the depredations of irresponsible guerrillas were a constant source of anxiety ; but their greatest loss came from the almost total cessation of business."

"When peace was restored, Elder Eads applied himself with great energy, and successfully, to repair the damages his people had suffered. But he was pained to see them steadily decline in numbers. The effect of the war

COMMUNITY AT SOUTH UNION, KY.

had been disastrous, not only financially, but it seemed also to have changed the public sense of religious and moral obligation to a feeling of indifference and lukewarmness, and his efforts to counteract this tendency were unceasing. He devotedly preached and lectured, and kept his pen busy to promote the cause to which he was pledged, and it did seem at times as if he would succeed. He formed a numerous company from Sweden into a family, and erected new buildings to accommodate the increasing number of novices ; but alas ! but few endured the period of probation before they fell back into 'the weak and beggarly elements' of the world. These disappointments did not crush his heroic spirit. And he set himself to fulfill literally the Master's behest, and gathered all manner of folk from the highways and hedges, the streets and lanes, if peradventure a few among them might be found wearing 'the wedding garment,' worthy to eat bread in the kingdom of God. It is not given to any man to say that the labors of the latter years of his life were wholly fruitless ; if the immediate result of his unselfish efforts has been small, the just records of eternity will undoubtedly reveal that much of the seed he has sown has not been wasted."

"Throughout his long and useful life he was a firm advocate of the principles of religious communism and celibacy, and what he taught he embodied in his conduct. He dignified hand labor and practiced it to the last. The versatility of mind which led him to become thoroughly grounded in theology, science, and mathematics, and enabled him to acquire a good working knowledge of several languages, also extended into the region of commerce, mechanics, and agriculture : indeed, he seemed to have a good share of that practical ingenuity which distinguished his near relative, Capt. Eads, the famous engineer. When, not many years ago, instrumental music was introduced and none was found capable of playing piano or organ, with characteristic energy he applied himself to the task of studying music, and soon was able to instruct younger people in the art. His contributions to the Western press were quite numerous, but the work by which he is best known and will be longest remembered is 'Shaker Theology : Scripto-Rational,' an octavo of three hundred pages, which has passed through several editions. His character was of puritanical sternness ; he was a strict disciplinarian and insisted upon obedience to the rules of Shaker life—'the sacred laws of Zion,' as he was wont to term them. He 'magnified his office,' and held it as a sacred trust for which he was accountable ; yet personally he was of a very kindly and affectionate disposition, easily approached by children or any one, and his conversation sparkled with quaint old-time humor. He was as happy as any one could be in his environment. What to the great majority of mankind appears to be but an abject servitude was to him a means whereby to gain true liberty—a life he had chosen voluntarily, and the full value of which he had experienced. "

"He now has stepped behind the veil ; but he will not be a stranger there, for many of those whom he has led into the higher life and who have gone before him will stand ready with celestial greetings, welcoming him to the kingdom of Him whose servant he was. His own people loved and revered him, and the world honored and respected him. The Louisville Courier-Journal, when printing his farewell sermon in August last, spoke of him as 'one of the purest and best of men.' Can a nobler epitaph than that be written of any man?"

CHAPTER XII.

COMMUNITY AT BUSRO—INDIAN RAIDS—WAR—SHAKERS DRAFTED— BILL PASSED FOR THEIR RELIEF.

AS an outcome of the Kentucky revival, a Community of Shakers was established for a time in the village of Busro, on the Wabash river, a settlement on the extreme frontier, then the Indian Territory. In 1811 the Believers at Mount Lebanon sent out to this distant post Issachar Bates, Archibald Meacham, and others, as missionaries. On their arrival, in the spring of the same year, they found some two hundred persons believers in the faith of Ann Lee. Issachar and Archibald immediately began the work of organizing a Shaker Society in this wilderness. They vigorously laid the axe at the root of the trees enlarging the clearing which had already been started, ploughed the land, planted seed, built log houses, and in the fall were rewarded by a plentiful harvest, which was readily disposed of in the surrounding district, often in gifts to many unfortunates suffering for want of food. During the winter and spring, a saw and grist mill were in process of erection; meanwhile, some one hundred and fifty others had joined the Society and everything was progressing favorably for the Shaker settlement, when the rumors of an Indian war broke upon the serenity of the followers of Mother Ann.

General William Henry Harrison was the governor of the Indiana Territory, and to him had been intrusted the control of all Indian affairs by President Madison. Matched against General Harrison was the proud and defiant Tecumseh, the head chief of all the Indian tribes.

As a precautionary measure, Governor Harrison called out the militia, and the Shaker Community were notified to join the army at once, which summons, as followers of the Prince of Peace, they willfully disregarded. In the meantime the lordly Tecumseh had been summoned to appear before His Excellency Governor Harrison, at Vincennes. Tecumseh, with a large following of his warriors, appeared in person before the Governor, disclaiming any intention of war against the whites. And so the counsel came to an end, with the only result of a deep distrust on both sides. Farms were abandoned, and there was a general flocking into the forts by the people, who believed an Indian war was imminent.

About the middle of June, a party of Indians visited the Shakers, bringing a quantity of farming tools with them to be repaired. Elder Issachar, fearful of a condemnation by the Governor if the work was done without his permission, wrote to him for instructions, and received in reply that no smithwork whatever should be done for the Indians; only to feed them well and treat them kindly. The Indians were greatly disappointed at this turn in affairs, and declared they had no thought of war. As they were accompanied by their wives and children, it would appear that there was a measure of truth in their assertion: "We don't take our squaws with us when we are on the war path."

For nearly a month, some two hundred of the redskins were encamped near the Shaker settlement, and as they behaved very peaceably, and took their departure without making a single inroad upon the property of the Shaker fraternity, it lent color to the report that the Shakers were in league with the Indians for the expulsion of the whites. This was further strengthened by the absolute refusal of the Shakers to take up arms against the Indians, and led some of the more hot-headed opposers of Shakerism to declare that Elder Issachar and his followers were at the bottom of all the trouble, and should be banished forthwith from the territory. In the very height of all this excitement, a malarial fever of malignant type broke out among the Brethren, which prostrated a very large number of them. A strolling band of Indians improved this opportunity to secure a valuable team of horses belonging to the Shakers, and one night crept down to the stable and captured the best four-horse team in all that section, and made off with them. The Shakers were loath to lose so many valuable horses without an effort for their recovery, so a couple of the Brethren, with one Capt. Robbins, a friendly world's man, followed up the Indian trail for nearly a hundred miles, and succeeded in capturing the horses and started on their return trip. They had proceeded less than ten miles when they were overtaken by the same Indians, who not only recaptured the four horses, but took with them the three that Abraham, James and Capt. Robbins had ridden in their journey. Capt. Robbins was indignant that his companions would willingly submit to such treatment without fighting for their rights; and he implored them strongly to allow him to hold the "red devils" at bay, but to no purpose; they would only answer him, "Nay, nay, friend Robbins, we must not commit so grievous a sin."

Whether or not Abraham and James met with a change of heart, on this particular point, during their long and tedious journey on foot homeward, Capt. Robbins never knew, and neither did he feel particularly comforted with the rejoicing of the Elders over their safe return, and all because they had so rigidly obeyed the injunction "not to fight under any circumstances.'

However, this affair tended, in a measure, to relieve the Shakers from the stigma, under which they were resting, that they were in league with the Indians for the overthrow of the whites, as it was seen that the Indians were no respecters of persons in their raids.

By the middle of September, the advance troops under General Harrison began to arrive at Busro, and a company of cavalry and two of infantry were quartered in the Shaker Village. The Elder's house was used as a store-house by the commissary, and the back door-yard appropriated as a slaughter pen, much to the disgust of the Elders; and to crown it all the beating drums and piercing fifes, turned the heretofore peaceful settlement into a camp of war. Many of the Shakers were drafted into the service, while all were required to do military duty, and for their non-attendance were mulcted with fines. Matters were going very hard against these Brethren of peace, when Capt. Boyd, with five hundred regulars from Boston, Mass., arrived. He at once interceded in behalf of the persecuted Shakers, saying that he knew them at the East to be of the best of people in the community. About the same time, Col. Davis arrived with a troop of cavalry from Kentucky. He being well acquainted with the Pleasant Hill Shakers in that State, was also friendly to them here, and joined Col. Boyd in his efforts to relieve the Shakers from doing military duty.

On the 26th of September, Gen. Harrison himself arrived, when all of the drafted Shakers were ordered to report for duty at twelve o'clock. By the advice of Col. Davis, who was a lawyer, the Shaker Elders called upon General Harrison and made known to him their situation, and it was finally arranged that the Shakers might remain in camp at their settlement and be detailed as hospital nurses, and such of the soldiery as were sick, were left behind under their care, while on the 28th the army took up their march northward to meet the foe.

It was not until the 5th of November that the famous battle of Tippecanoe was fought, and in which General Harrison routed the brave Tecumseh and laid in waste his town and all therein.

Some years after this event, owing to the continued unhealthy condition of Busro, arising from the malarial banks of the Wabash, the Shakers abandoned their settlement, removing to Ohio and Kentucky.

After General Harrison's defeat of the British in Canada, he retired to the State of Ohio, and was a member of the Legislature there in 1821, at which time he presented a petition for the relief of the Shakers in that state from military duty, substituting for them three day's work on the highway, in place of the three days of military duty, all able-bodied men were obliged to perform. This measure he advocated in four able speeches before the House, and it was largely due to his influence that the bill was passed.

At the present time, the Shaker Societies have Communities at Union Village, White Water and Watervliet, Ohio; Pleasant Hill and South Union, Kentucky.

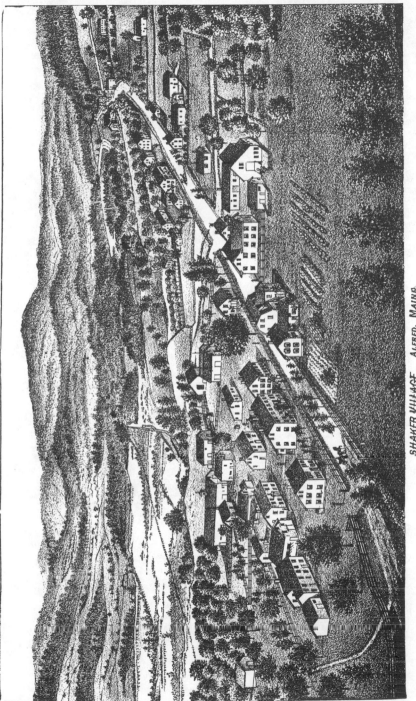

SHAKER VILLAGE, ALFRED, MAINE.

ELDRESS, MARY P. VANCE.

CHAPTER XIII.

MAINE—JOHN COTTON—"NEW LIGHTS"—"MERRY DANCERS"—
"COME-OUTERS"—"NEW-LIGHT BAPTISTS"—ELDRESSES
MARY P. VANCE AND MARY A. W. GILLISPIE.

THE history of the establishment of the Shakers in the State of Maine is akin to that of Kentucky, and there originated in the person of one John Cotton, a son of John Cotton whose name is mentioned in the history of the town of Gorham. John Cotton settled in Alfred, Me., about the year 1781. He married Eleanor Coffin, a daughter of Simeon Coffin, who is said to have been the first white man to penetrate the forest of what was then called by the Indians, Massabesic, and took up his abode in an Indian wigwam, which then stood near the site of the present Shaker house of worship in Alfred.

At the time of John Cotton's advent in Alfred, an extensive revival of religion was prevailing in the western part of that State, also in Vermont, New Hampshire and Massachusetts. The nature of the revival partook much of the form of Second Adventism, and many of the converts announced the speedy coming of Christ, the day of judgment, and the millennium as being at hand. Nearly, if not quite, all of the subjects were impelled to express their enthusiasm in singing and dancing, shaking off the fetters of the set forms and creeds of the old established churches, to make room for the "new light" which they proclaimed as about to dawn upon the earth. By the unbelieving portion of the community, these religious enthusiasts were known by the name of "New Lights," "Merry Dancers," "Come-outers," and "New-Light Baptists," by which latter name they became to be known wherever they had an existence. To this order John Cotton attached himself in 1781, and became a very zealous member.

In 1783, John Cotton caught the emigration fever then so prevalent for settling in Vermont. With John Coffin as a companion, the two started out on foot to make a new home for themselves in that State. Their long tramp led them through the towns of Canterbury and Enfield, N. H. Here, much to John's surprise, he found more of the New-Light Baptists. At Enfield he tarried for a few days with one of the advanced brothers in the new light doctrine, one James Jewett, a well-to-do farmer, who had adopted the faith of the Mother Ann proselytes from Mt. Lebanon. Among the many things which farmer James sought to impress upon his Christian guest, was the utter impossibility of living a pure, Christ-like, virgin life, in a state of matrimony. John tells us that this so worked upon his mind, that he became convinced of the truth of it, and then and there made a confession of his sins to James. John has also left his testimony, that, one morning after breakfast, when seated with James, talking upon this subject, he was raised from his chair by an all-controlling power and spun round like a top for the space of half an hour, when he was whirled through the open door and down to the waters of Mascoma Lake, some rods distant, and then was whirled back again with the same force and landed in the same chair he was taken from. This event, he says, he regarded as a seal to his faith and a baptism of the Holy Spirit which he determined to keep to the end of his days, and decided him to return to Alfred, which he did without delay. On arriving at his house, he related his remarkable experience, and prepared the way for the missionaries from Mt. Lebanon, N. Y., Enfield, N. H., and Hancock, Mass., who soon followed him.

Meetings were held in Alfred, Lyman, Waterborough, Gorham, Windham, New Gloucester, Poland and Falmouth, in what was then the Province of Maine.

In 1784, a company from Gorham and New Gloucester (Sabbath-Day Pond) chartered a small vessel at Portland, called "The Shark," to go to New York, thence up the Hudson river to Albany, with the avowed object of visiting Mother Ann and the Elders at Niskeyuna. Thirteen Brethren and twelve Sisters constituted the party for the pilgrimage, which was undertaken in the month of August, and safely accomplished, although they encountered a severe storm on their return trip, on the evening of Sept. 7th, just outside of New York harbor, which nearly resulted in their destruction, but from which they happily escaped without loss. Later on, in the same month, a company of ten Brethren and Sisters accomplished the same journey on horseback. The Society at Alfred, Me., was organized in March, 1793.

Doubtless, residing in the city of Lowell, Mass., there are many fashionable women who will recall to mind, in the cut displayed though disguised in the garb of a Sister Shaker, the pleasant face and affable manner of one who, twenty-five years ago, was at the head of the millinery establishment of one of the leading firms in that city, Mary P. Vance, now the senior Eldress on the Board of Elders in the Church Family of the United Society of Believers, commonly called Shakers, at Alfred, Me.

She was born in the town of Lebanon, York County, Me., on the 16th of November, 1845, the daughter of Shubael B. and Abigail (Hussey) Vance, and a grand-daughter of the late Hon. William Vance, of Readfield, Me. He was a large land-holder in the eastern part of that State, and was a member of the convention for forming the constitution of Maine, after its separation from Massachusetts.

At eight years of age, Mary's parents removed to Lowell, Mass., where

Eldress Mary A. Gillispie.

she received her education in the public schools until she arrived at the age of fifteen, when she entered one of the leading millinery establishments of Lowell, to learn that business, where she remained until October of the year 1864 ; the last two years as the manager of that department.

On several occasions before she was eighteen years of age, she made visits to her brother, John B. Vance, who was a member of the Society of Shakers at Alfred, Me ; and now an Elder in the Church Family of that body, and upon each occasion expressed a great and growing desire to join the fraternity.

This was most strenuously opposed by her mother, who fondly desired her to remain with them in Lowell and to accept the attentions of a young, estimable gentleman who sought her hand in marriage.

But in the month of October, 1864, she decided to sever her very pleasant connections in Lowell and join the Shakers, towards whom she had been so strongly drawn by the feeling that in no other way could she satisfy the craving demands of her conscience. So, at the age of nineteen, consecrating her little all to God and the good of humanity, she joined the Society of Believers at Alfred, and for the past twenty years has been a member of the Board of Elders there, of which she is now the senior Sister.

We are indebted to venerable Bishop Harvey Eads, of South Union, Ky., for the original of this excellent likeness of Sister Mary Vance. Bishop Eads, in his communication, says : "I send her photograph, because it is the best representation of Shaker costume of any in my album."

The late Mary Ann Gillispie, who was long an associate on the same board with Sister Mary P. Vance, will also be remembered by many of those who have visited the Shakers in Alfred. She was born in Portsmouth, N. H., on the 9th of June, 1829. Her father, Joseph Gillispie, was an English sea captain ; her mother, Mary Ann (Wendall) Gillispie, died when her daughter was but four years of age, leaving her in the care of a kind friend, who was as a mother to her until she arrived at the age of eleven years, when the failing health of her adopted mother resulted in the removal of the child to be further cared for by the Shakers in Canterbury, N. H. Here her spirituality and amiability soon won for her the position of caretaker for a company of little girls. At the age of twenty-three she had advanced to the position of one of the presiding Elders over the Novitiate, or North Family, as it was then called. After eight years of faithful service here, she was still further advanced as the assistant to Hester Ann Adams on the board of Elders of the Ministry, at Alfred and New Gloucester, Me. Here, for twenty-seven years she faithfully served this people, until her labors on earth ceased, on the 15th of April, 1887. Of her it was well said that during all these years she was an able minister of the truth, her life emphasizing her teachings, her heart so filled with the love of humanity that very many outside of the pale of Shakerism felt her loss in the Community.

CHAPTER XIV.

SHAKER MISSION INTO MAINE—ALFRED COMMUNITY—BOYHOOD
VANITY OF FATHER JOHN BARNES—"THOMPSON'S POND PLAN-
TATION"—NEW GLOUCESTER COMMUNITY—"THE RANG"—
SABBATHDAY LAKE—POLAND MINERAL SPRINGS—
GREAT LONGEVITY OF THE SHAKERS.

FATHER JAMES WHITTAKER made his first and only visit into the
State, or what was then called the Province of Maine, in the summer of
1785. He was accompanied by Elders, Henry Clough, Job Bishop, Eleazer
Rand and Ebenezer Cooley. Their mission was extended as far east as Gorham. Meetings were held all along the route, and large audiences gathered
to hear the Shaker doctrine expounded. Often a spirit of opposition manifested itself against Father James, who was not mild in denouncing the sins
of the flesh, which irritated in no small degree a majority of those present.

On one occasion, when preaching a very plain and pointed sermon at Gorham, Father James was interrupted several times by the village black and
white smith, one Richard Edwards, who, being a man of powerful frame, was
regarded by the populace as the champion of all their rights; and perhaps,
somewhat in the character of the blustering bully of the neighborhood, he
sought to strike terror into the heart of James by his frequent interruptions.
But there generally comes a time in the life of every man of this stamp when
he stands aghast at the temerity of some less stalwart individual, and bows
his head in shame, as did Edwards on this occasion, when the brave old sea
captain, John Stevenson, commanded him to sit down. "Sit down, Edwards," he said, "hold your tongue, and let this man preach. You may
know how to make a plow, or an ox yoke, but, hang me, if you know how to
preach. We came to hear this man Whittaker preach, not to listen to your
silly gabble." Every one present felt that the old captain spoke to be obeyed,
and there was no more disturbance.

From Gorham Father James returned to Alfred, a few miles distant, and
from thence, shortly after, to the Societies in Massachusetts.

The first house built for public worship in Alfred by the Shakers, was
raised in the summer of 1786, but it was never wholly finished. Twelve
rough-hewn beams, twelve inches square, cut from the clearest of pine timber, were exposed to view overhead.

The Shaker Society at Alfred, Me., was organized in March, 1793, under
the charge of Father John Barnes, of Alfred; Elder Robert McFarland, of

NOVITIATE ORDER, POLAND HILL.

COMMUNITY AT GLOUCESTER, ME.

Gorham ; Mother Sarah Kendall and Eldress Lucy Prescott, both of Harvard, Mass. These two Sister Shakers rode in the saddle—which was the almost universal mode of travel at that date—from Harvard to Alfred, and were the first Shaker Sisters to visit the Province of Maine. On leaving Harvard, they were presented with the horses, saddles and bridles, and bidden God speed by those left behind.

Of the worldly vanity of Father John Barnes in his younger days, a good story is still extant. It is said that upon one occasion, when Mother Ann and the Elders were on a visit at Harvard, Mass., from their home at Niskeyuna, John was very eager to meet with Mother Ann, and so strong was the desire that he made the journey on horseback from Alfred to Harvard for that purpose. Arriving at Harvard, he put up at the village inn and retired to a room, from which he shortly emerged dressed in broadcloth, knee-breeches, long black stockings with silver buckles, a profusion of lace and ruffles in his shirt bosom and cuffs, with a blue silk stock about his neck, a low crowned fur hat on his head, with a walking-stick in his hand, and sallied forth, bent upon making the striking impression upon Mother Ann that in himself was embodied the elements of true Shakerism.

Arriving at the house to which he had been directed, just as a Brother Shaker was emerging therefrom, he inquired if the "Lady Elect" was within. The brother gazed on him from head to foot with amazement. At last, finding his tongue, he replied : "I presume the woman to whom thou hast made reference is within. If thou desirest to see her, walk up to the door and knock."

As he halted upon the steps and stooped to brush the dust from his well-polished boots with his silk kerchief, Mother Ann came to the door. With a scornful glance, she said : "You proud and haughty young man, kneel where you are, humble yourself before your God, and pray to Him to give you a spirit of humility." John, completely overcome by the force of her rebuke, which he felt most keenly, sank upon his knees, profusely apologizing for his vanity.

Realizing that John was sincere in his desire for reformation, Mother Ann invited him into the house, and cared for him as for a son. He prolonged his visit for several days. Meanwhile, making his confession to Elder William Lee, he became established in the simple faith of Shakerism.

In the early days of Shakerism at Alfred, Me., very many of the converts claimed the power of healing the sick and of prophesying, all of which, no doubt, confirmed the people in their faith and added many to the Church. As an instance of their enthusiasm, a case is cited in which one William Nason, a very upright and conscientious man, felt called upon to warn the people to keep the fear of God constantly before their eyes, marched in the road which encompassed Massabesic Lake, a distance of some four miles, repeating at frequent intervals : "Woe ! woe to the inhabitants of the earth ! Touch not my anointed, and do my good prophets no harm."

It was not an uncommon thing for the world's people to overhear in the early morning one Shaker brother salute his nearest Shaker neighbor with the words, "More love, brother David," and then for the person addressed to reply, "More love, brother William." Then a more distant Shaker brother, hearing the salutation, would take up the refrain, "More love, brother John," until for a long distance the air would resound with the Shaker melody as it came from scores of the devoted followers of Ann Lee.

To-day the Shaker Community at Alfred, Me., have in their possession some twelve hundred acres of land, beautifully situated on very elevated ground, known as Shaker Hill. Upon the top of this hill stands the little Shaker Village consisting of about twenty-four old-fashioned farm houses, most of them having been built nearly one hundred years ago. They are in excellent repair, each building standing by itself, with an extensive green lawn stretching out on all sides. One line of these houses is fronting on the main street, while another straight row stands in the rear. This Society is divided into what are called two families, containing in all about seventy-five persons.

Elder John B. Vance is the recognized head of this Society. While their occupation is mostly that of tilling the land, every needful occupation for their support is carried on in the village. They have a fine stream of water which courses through the valley below, on which stands the mill which grinds the grain harvested from the large acreage under cultivation.

After the organization of the Shaker Society in Alfred, Me., in 1793, the meeting house of 1786 was found to be inadequate for the accommodation of the Believers, and a more commodious one was built, after the model of the Mount Lebanon Church, the same being finished in 1794, and stands to-day as a monument of the dispensation granted by Father Joseph Meacham in these words: "If you, as a people, believe it to be your duty to build a house to meet in, as you have signified, you have liberty, according to the same order and covenant our own here in New Lebanon was built." The conditions were as follows:

1. That it should be built by free contributions. No one must be asked to give anything; all donations must be made freely, and as a matter of their own faith, and by their gift no one must be brought into debt or blame on account of their donation. God required of no man more than he was able to do in justice, thus leaving it to every Brother to be the judge of his own circumstances.

2. That it should be done by a joint union and agreement with each other.

3. As the house was to be for religious, and not for common use, none should hold a right of government in the house by virtue of what they had done, but by Church order, the property being changed from a private to a public use, is consecrated to the Lord. It shall be the privilege of all that believe, and are holden in union, according to their opportunity, to assemble therein, one day in seven, for the public worship of God. Any further use

Sabbathday Lake, at Gloucester, Me.

of the house than this must be by order, as the good of the Church and Society may require.

If all of the churches erected by other denominations were built with the same Christian spirit, church debts would be unknown, and the line less sharply drawn, even if it did not wholly disappear, between the rich and the poor.

The new meeting house was constructed with apartments for the accommodation of the Ministry, which were not only ample for themselves, but for all who might chance to come from other Societies. Very many of those who had professed the Shaker faith in the surrounding towns, sold their possessions and removed to Alfred. Flax was raised by the Shakers every year in considerable quantity. This was carded and spun into yarn, and manufactured into cloth by the Sisters, who occupied several rooms with their spinning-wheels and looms, in a building erected in 1796 as a Sisters' shop. This workshop still stands, having been put in thorough repair in 1872.

The Shaker Sisters displayed no little skill in their handicraft, in making kerchiefs of fine linen, some in white borders, and others checked in blue and white. Sheep were raised for their wool, and cotton was bought in Portland, and it was no uncommon thing for the Sisters to work far into the night in the carding and spinning of cotton, wool and flax, manufacturing the same into cloth, not only for the use of the Shaker fraternity, but for the general market. Even after the introduction of machinery in Rhode Island for the making of cotton yarn, merchants in Portland would supply the Society with the yarn, which the Sisters would weave into cloth at a certain price per yard.

The old meeting house of 1786, was transformed into a workshop for the men, who there manufactured, on quite a large scale, tubs, pails, churns, spinning-wheels, and other articles of a domestic nature.

The establishment of the Shaker Society at New Gloucester, Me., was brought about by the advent of Elisha Pote, Nathan Merrill and Joseph Stone, who came from Gorham, Me., in the month of November, 1782, into what was then called "Thompson's Pond Plantation," and tarried at the house of one Gowan Wilson, senior, where they held meetings and expounded the doctrine of Shakerism to those who gathered in to learn of the new and strange religion from the lips of Elisha Pote whose gift of oratory had spread well over that sparsely settled community.

These meetings consisted of singing, preaching and dancing, and a general invitation was extended to all present to unite with them in the exercises. Among the very first to avail themselves of this privilege were Dorothy Pote and Mary Merrill, who simultaneously became inspired with an impulse which agitated them violently. They soon began to turn swiftly and spin like tops which was continued for the space of an hour, much to the amazement of the Gentiles who were present.

This influence rapidly spread among the people of that neighborhood and very many became proselytes, regarding the ambassadors as harbingers of God, the doctrine of Mother Ann Lee as the complete embodiment of the true Christian religion, and that through her, Christ had surely made his second appearance on earth.

Early to embrace this faith were some of the most prominent families in that section. Among the number were Gowan Wilson, in whose house the meetings were held; Nathan, and Edmund and also James Merrill with his daughter Mary; Josiah, Simeon and Gersham Holmes; Thomas Pote, the father of Elisha; Samuel Pote, Elisha's elder brother, with their sister Dorothy; Barnabas and Ephraim Briggs; Thomas Cushman and Eliphaz Ring, the latter residing on "Rang" Hill, one of three hills lying side by side, adjacent to three ponds similarly situated. The hills and ponds ranging side by side, this locality came to be known as the "Rang," the old settlers pronouncing the word as if rhyming with bang.

The first converts were made on the 24th of November, 1782. Eliphaz Ring then owned the farm on which is now located the celebrated Mineral spring property of Hiram Ricker and Sons in Poland. At first, these new converts personally held their own property, but, later on, they adopted the community scheme and held all things in common. It was from the great liberality of Eliphaz that the Shakers at Alfred became possessed of their valuable water privilege and mills.

In 1793, Jabez Ricker, the grandfather of Hiram, the senior in the firm of the present proprietors of the Mineral spring property, exchanged his farm in Alfred, Me., where he then resided, for the Ring property. Eliphaz, with others, then removed to Alfred, and was one of the number to assist in establishing the Society there.

The organization of the Shaker Community in New Gloucester was accomplished on the 19th of April, 1794, under the leadership of Father John Barnes, from the Society at Alfred. His associates were Elder Robert McFarland, from Gorham, Me., and Mother Sarah Kendall and Eldress Lucy Prescott, from the Society at Harvard, Mass. These persons comprised the established Ministry for the Societies at Gorham and Alfred, and the new organization at West Gloucester, the name given to the settlement at "Thompson's Pond Plantation."

The Ministry appointed Nathan Merrill and Barnabas Briggs as Trustees of the West Gloucester Society. Their first meeting house was raised on the fourteenth of the following June. The design was after the old Dutch style of houses of worship then in vogue in New York. The timber for the meeting house and central dwelling had been cut, drawn to the spot and framed, some two years previous. The twenty thousand bricks in the huge chimneys of the central dwelling, were made near the foot of the "Pond." They were somewhat smaller in size than are those of the present day. All

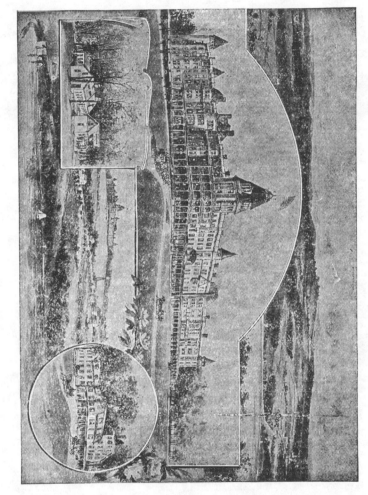

POLAND HILL SPRINGS.

the nails used in the construction of the two buildings were forged by hand by one of the Shaker brothers, Joseph Briggs, a son of Ephraim, and his young apprentice. The church building was finished and ready for occupancy on Christmas day of that same year.

The new organization was composed of individuals of very moderate circumstances. Their combined acreage in land formed, at first, but a meagre means for support, but by prudence, industry and good management, they have succeeded in amassing a valuable property, consisting of nearly two thousand acres of land.

In 1819, the Gorham Society removed to "Poland Hill," the first and highest of the "Rang," which is situated one mile north of the New Gloucester Society, and united with it, forming the Novitiate Order for this Community. This Society retained the name of West Gloucester, until less than three years since. In 1890 the change was made to that of Sabbathday Lake. The main reason for this change was on account of the numerous blunders occasioned by the transmission of their mail, which very often made the journey to West Gloucester, Mass., before arriving at its proper destination.

In olden times, when the Indians were the sole occupants of this section of the Province of Maine, a party of pale-faced explorers came upon this lovely spot in the wilderness—the three beautiful sheets of water hidden at the foot of the tri-mountain hills, and another larger sheet at the south-east. Being infatuated with the charming beauty of the place, they decided to make this their general camping ground, and on week-days, to range over the surrounding country, camping at night wherever the shades of evening might overtake them, but on Sunday they were all to meet on the shores of the larger pond for consultation and social chat. From this circumstance the locality came to be known as "Sabbathday Pond." So when it was decided to change the name of West Gloucester Post Office, that of Sabbathday Pond was suggested. But, as Uncle Sam was already blessed with a "Sabbathday Point" Post Office, it was thought that the object sought in the change might be defeated by reason of the great similarity of the two names, therefore that of Sabbathday Lake was chosen, which certainly has the merit of being more euphonious, to say the least, and as no further trouble has occurred in the miscarriage of the mails, the object sought for has been accomplished.

Two miles further to the north of this quiet Shaker village is the old Eliphaz Ring farm and the celebrated Poland Mineral Spring, which is now said to have one of the largest and best equipped barreling and bottling establishments in the United States.

Situated upon the middle "Rang" of the three hills, upon the old Eliphaz Ring farm plateau, eight hundred feet above the level of the sea, stands that palace of hotels, "The Poland Spring House," in the midst of some of the most beautiful scenery for which Maine is so noted. This hostelry, with the equally well known and favorite "Old Mansion House," has become one of the most fashionable of all the New England resorts, and is well filled in the summer months with a constant moving multitude who are drawn thither to quaff of the refreshing and curative properties of the mineral waters from the Poland Spring and feast from the delectable bounties of the table our host Ricker spreads for his guests.

This great influx of strangers is made a source of no little profit to the Shakers of Sabbathday Lake, who find at the hotels, and their own village store, a good market for their fancy work of "Fir-balsam" pillows, filled from the luxuriant fir trees of old-growth pines which are still standing on their property; for their tiny, whisking hat brushes, made of horse-hair, and finished in velvet and ribbon of bright colors; for their fancy Shaker baskets, and plush rugs and bouquets of flowers; for the thousand and one little articles so deftly made, and which are carried away to grace the homes of departing visitors, as mementos of the handiwork of this most singular and upright people, the Shakers.

That the life and habits of the Shakers are conducive to longevity has been proved beyond cavil. A careful examination of the death records at Sabbathday Lake, covering a period of one hundred and six years, from 1787 to 1893, shows that the average age attained by the members of this Community to be fifty-eight and one-half years. This great prolonging of the average duration of life, far beyond that of any other class in the world, can not be wholly attributed to the magical effects of the waters of the Poland medicinal spring, notwithstanding their close proximity to the same, for we find the same conditions existing—the same extension of the span of life—in every Shaker Community wherever situated.

CHAPTER XV.

CANTERBURY COMMUNITY—CONCORD—WATTANUMMON'S FIELD—
DONATION OF BENJAMIN AND MARY WHITCHER—FATHER
JOB BISHOP—PETER AYERS—DAVID PARKER, TRUSTEE—
ELDER HENRY C. BLINN—SR. MARY WHITCHER.

THE Society of Shakers at Canterbury, N. H., is located on gracefully rising ground, overlooking most of the surrounding country, high up on the Canterbury hills, twelve miles north-east of that beautiful City of Elms—Concord, the capital of the State.

To a person shut up within the walls of city life, who longs to breathe the pure air of heaven, no more enjoyable trip could be planned for an outing than a ride over the hills from Concord to Canterbury. Passing out from the city between the noble elms which line each side of Main street, forming a perfect arch in summer, to the north end, or head of Main street, by the old ancient landmark, the Rev. Timothy Walker estate, the first lot in the first range laid out in Penacook* (Concord,) in 1726. Here on the brow of Horseshoe Pond Hill, lived Parson Walker, in a log house, until 1733-4, when he built the two-story gambrel-roofed house, which is said to be the oldest two-story dwelling house between Haverhill, Mass., and Canada. This house, with some modern improvement, still stands surrounded by the stately elm trees set out by Mr. Walker's own hand in 1756, and is now owned and occupied by his great grandson, Hon. Joseph B. Walker, as his residence.

Passing these beautiful grounds, we make a sharp turn to the right, down the hill, crossing the tracks of the two branches of the Boston and Maine Railway divisions of the Contoocook Valley and Northern railroads, we strike into the Interval road skirting Horseshoe Pond, once the ancient bed of the Merrimack River now a mile distant.

At this point we see within the Horseshoe vast acres of green grass called Horseshoe Island, and a little further on is Wattanummon's Field, still known and called such, after an Indian chief of this name, who, at the time of the arrival of the first settlers, was living in a wigwam on the little rise of ground just over the brook, which is the outlet of the pond into the Merrimack, and over which we are about to cross by a stone bridge, called Wattanummon's Bridge.

A well preserved tradition respecting Wattanummon's dominion over this field is extant, and almost any old farmer in that locality will tell you of the advent of Captain Ebenezer Eastman and his men, in the summer of 1726, into Wattanummon's field to cut the grass, when the old Indian chief and two of his sons sallied forth with their guns to prevent the trespass. Eastman and his party, seeing the warlike approach of the land claimants, laid aside their scythes and waved a flag of truce in the shape of the demijohn, the contents of which were so well known to the Indian. When within speaking distance, the brave Wattanummon called out in his broken English; "My land! my land! no cut! no cut!" and raised up his gun as if to shoot. Eastman hastened to reply; "Yes, this is your land—your grass. Won't you come and take a drink with me, and we will talk it over?" The old Indian drew himself up with dignity as he took the proffered cup, and said;

---

* A powerful tribe of Indians, known as the Penacooks, were found occupants of the soil which is now Concord, by the first white explorers in that region in 1638. This territory was known as the Plantation of Penacook from 1725 to 1733. It was then incorporated as the township of Rumford, which name it retained until 1765, when it became incorporated under the name of Concord.

"Yes, yes; me drink first;" and drained the cup to the last drop. Eastman then poured out another cup for one of the sons, when the chief interposed, saying; "He little, he no drink;" and taking the cup, drank it himself, exclaiming; "Ugh, it good! it good! Yes, my land! my grass! all mine; everything mine!" Then, as the warming contents of his draught began to tell upon his generous nature, he loftily stretched forth his arms, exclaiming; "My grass, all your grass! You good white man, have him all!" Which liberal offer Eastman hastened to bind with another cup of rum from the jug, which he presented to the chief in exchange for grass.

Crossing the Merrimack a little further on, and the tracks of the Boston, Concord and Montreal Railroad, we find ourselves in the pretty little village of East Concord, which, less than sixty years ago bid fair to be the most central portion of the town, owing to the manufacturing interests then expected to be built by the Sewall's Falls Locks and Canal Corporation which had nearly completed a dam across the Merrimack, and had constructed a canal two miles in length through this part of the town. But the failure of the enterprise in the panic of 1837, dashed the hopes and depleted the pockets of some of the strongest advocates of the scheme, to such an extent that they were willing to retire from the contest. However, recently the subject of building a dam across the river at the same spot has again been agitated, and a company has been organized, with George F. Page as president to promote the enterprise. As Mr. Page is one of the largest stock-holders in the company, and is well known as the very popular president of the Page Belting Company in Concord, the enterprise is looked upon as a pronounced success, and the citizens are looking forward with much interest to the establishment of the Concord Electrical Light Works, as well as other manufacturing interests in that part of the city.

From this point on, for ten miles to the Shaker village, we pass up a gradual rise of land until we reach the Shaker settlement. On the way, we pass some of the best farms in the Granite State. The Shaker village itself has a wonderfully clean and neat appearance. The houses, church, school building, workshops, barns, stables and sheds are kept in the best of repair, showing unmistakable evidence in every department that the followers of Ann Lee are grounded in the faith that "cleanliness is next to godliness."

The Canterbury Society was organized in 1792, Benjamin Whitcher having generously donated his fine farm of one hundred acres of land, then valued at two thousand one hundred and fifty dollars, to the Community. He, with his wife, Mary Shepard, had located at an early date on that spot in the then wilderness of Canterbury, on the tract of land which was purchased for him by his father, Benjamin Whitcher, in 1774. It was several years before they had any neighbors—none within a distance of several miles. In time a meeting house was built, located but two miles from their home, but, following out the established order of those days, it was of the Congregational de-

VIEW OF CANTERBURY, N. H.

Trustee's Office, East Canterbury, N. H.

nomination, for the support of which the law of the State taxed every family whether they were believers in the doctrine preached or not. The refusal of any to pay the taxes assessed, was followed by the visit of the sheriff, or his deputy, and the seizure of any property of the delinquent in sufficient amount to cover the debt and all costs of collection, was made, oftentimes to the great hardship of the unfortunate. But as this was all done for the promotion of the gospel and the support of the minister, those refusing or neglecting this divine order of things were regarded by the established church as reprobates of the lowest type.

We are told that the remarkable revival of religion which passed like a tidal wave over the New England States in 1776, paved the way for the acceptance by Benjamin and Mary Whitcher of the doctrine of Mother Ann Lee.

On the formation of the Society, Benjamin Whitcher was appointed one of the presiding Elders, while his wife was chosen as one of the directors of the temporal interests of the Community.

Prominent among the founders of the Canterbury Community was Father Job Bishop, who, in 1817, on the occasion of the visit of President James Monroe to the Enfield Society, on his tour through New England, made him this characteristic Shaker speech, which has gone down into history: "I, Job Bishop, welcome James Monroe to our habitation."

Associated with him was the venerable Peter Ayres, who died at the advanced age of ninety-seven in 1857, and whose quaint donation to the Shakers is made mention of on page 29; also Elder Henry Clough and John Wadleigh, the old unpensioned Revolutionary veteran, who was present and engaged in the memorable battle of Bunker Hill, on the 17th of June, 1775. He was a soldier of the Revolution for five years; was at the surrender of Fort Ticonderoga, in 1775, at the surrender of Burgoyne in October, 1777; in the Rhode Island expedition of 1778, and at the surrender of Cornwallis, at Yorktown, Va., October 19, 1781. But, true to his Shaker faith, which he espoused in 1789, he positively refused to apply for, or to receive, any pension from the government for his services in the army, to which he was entitled by the laws of our country.

In 1814, a number of Shakers were drafted to perform military duty, but refused to serve. They were thereupon arrested and brought to trial. They pleaded their own cause, and so successfully, that all but three were discharged. The three unfortunates, in order to meet the requirements of the law, were fined a moderate sum. Even this the Shakers refused to comply with, solely on the ground that it was against the fundamental principles of their religion to countenance war either directly or indirectly. For this refusal to comply with the laws of the nation they suffered imprisonment. However, at the close of the war, the President, by special proclamation, remitted the fines, and in 1816 the State of New York passed laws exempting the Shakers from doing military duty in time of peace.

Again, in our late Civil War, quite a large number of Shakers were drafted for service, but upon appealing to President Lincoln for exemption, an order was issued by the Secretary of War furloughing them "until called for."

That the Shakers, collectively and individually, remained true to their faith, may be seen in the records of the Pension Department, which show more than a half million dollars now standing to the credit of certain soldiers in the war of the Rebellion, who, after the close of the war were made converts to the faith of Mother Ann Lee and joined the Society of Shakers, but have refused to accept the money standing to their credit, on the ground that they could not stain their hands with the proceeds of funds given as a premium for services rendered in a cause so foreign to their ideas of humility and love towards all mankind.

With the Canterbury (N. H.) Society of Shakers I have long been familiar. My earliest recollections of them date back to my childhood. Well do I remember the kindly face of that genial prince of Shakers, David Parker, whom everybody knew, as the chief manager of the Community at Shaker Village in Canterbury; of his business visits upon my father at some seasons of the year almost every week; of his pleasantly chucking me under the chin when a lad of no more than four years of age; and of his asking me if I didn't want to go with him and grow up a Shaker. And my memory of the Shakers becomes more vivid as I recall the Second Advent craze which passed over New England a little later on, and caused so large a number of worthy individuals, believers in the "Miller doctrine," to neglect all worldly business and give themselves up solely to religious services; of their giving away all their earthly possessions; of their assembling in the old churchyard cemetery in Concord, N. H., on the memorable day of the 23d of April, 1843, clothed in white raiments, to witness the second advent of the Son of Man in the heavens, and by him to be caught up in the air with the rising "dead in the Lord," as the graves would open at the blast of Gabriel's trumpet, and they depart with him to everlasting joy, leaving behind the earth and all things earthly to be destroyed with unquenchable fire. Alas! poor deluded souls! the day and night passed with no unusual occurrence.

David Parker, in his day, was doubtless one of the most widely known of all the Shakers. He was remarkable for his industry, thrift and shrewdness, but combined with absolute honesty, which stamped him with the reputation of being perfectly reliable in every business transaction. He was born in Boston, Mass., on the 12th of May, 1807, and at the early age of ten was admitted to the Shaker Society in Canterbury. Here he received a good, thorough and practical education. That he improved his opportunities, and had more than ordinary ability, was made manifest when nine years later, at the age of nineteen, he received the appointment of assistant trustee. From that time till the date of his death, on the 20th of January, 1867, he was known as one of the most active and honorable business men in the State.

David Parker, Trustee.

Mary Whitcher, Trustee.

In May, 1837, he was appointed to the ministerial order of the Shakers. In October, 1846, he was again called to take charge of the financial interests of the Community. It was from his efforts before the Legislature of New Hampshire, at Concord, in the summer of 1848, that the inquisitorial arraignment of the Shakers which had been instigated by some who at a former period had been members of the fraternity, fell flat. On this occasion he acquitted himself as an able advocate in defense of that institution, against the vilest of insinuations as well as the direct defamatory charges of his accusers. At his urgent solicitation, a committee of the Legislature was appointed, delegated with the power to make a most searching investigation into every department of their private life, sacred order and spiritual records. This committee reported that they had been accorded every facility for a most thorough investigation and that the standard of morality among the Shakers was of the highest type, and they honorably acquitted them of all the charges brought against them. Other well known, prominent Shakers of a quarter of a century ago will be brought to mind, by the residents of New Hampshire, on the mention of the names of such Shaker brothers as Francis Winkley, Israel Sanborn, Caleb M. Dyer, Elder John Lyon, and also of Thomas Corbett, the originator of the celebrated, Corbett's Shaker Sarsaparilla, which has been manufactured by the Society for more than half a century, all of whom have long since passed over the river, but in their day and generation were not surpassed in ability, and integrity in the community by any citizens. To-day, Shakerism is well represented by such men as Elder F. W. Evans, the great expounder of Shaker doctrines, at Mount Lebanon, N. Y., Elders J. S. Kaime, H. C. Blinn, and N. A. Briggs at Canterbury, with many others we might mention.

The Community of Shakers at Canterbury consists of two families, the "Church," and the "Upper," or novitiate family. The name, "upper" family is merely a local application to designate it as to its situation in the village.

In the route from Concord, the Church Family is the first reached. Here is located the Trustees' Office, the Post Office, the Printing Office, schoolhouse and church.

Visitors alight at the Trustees' Office, and are ushered into a very homelike reception room; the floor is covered with a coat of yellow paint and well varnished, with here and there rag-braided carpet mats under the chairs and for the feet; a library near at hand, well filled with books; a washstand, water and towels in the corner; wooden blinds hung to the windows in such a manner as to exclude all light or the inclemency of the weather. Not a fly or an insect, apparently, ever enters herein; not a speck of dust or dirt, giving to this room a satisfying air of comfort truly refreshing. And later on, as we visit the other departments of the home of this peculiar people, we see everywhere this same degree of comfort, order and neatness.

The buildings are arranged on each side of the village street, enclosed by neat, substantial fences. At the Printing Office, the place of issue of *The Manifesto*, the Shaker monthly magazine, so ably edited by Elder Henry C. Blinn, we find Shaker maidens handling the type for the next issue, with the same swift movements which are characteristic of the city printing office. As we enter the "editor's den," we almost fancy that we have struck a department of Barnum's old museum once on Broadway, on the site of the *Herald* building. Lying all about the room, yet in perfect Shaker order, are old-fashioned curiosities of every name and description—spinning looms, warming pans, clay pipes and smoking tongs; the old iron candlestick of the past and the brass ones of later date, including the veritable old pitch-pine knot, which may have lighted, long ago, some poor old soul in the way of truth and Shakerism. In fact, Elder Blinn has made and well arranged a large collection of the relics of the past. His collection of minerals is also exceedingly interesting.

Elder Henry C. Blinn was born in the city of Providence, R. I., July 16, 1824. He joined the Shakers at Canterbury at the age of fourteen. He has passed through all the orders of Shakerism, and has been appointed to all the positions of trust that the faithful Shaker can be honored with in that Community. Some years ago he was made the editor of *The Manifesto*, a monthly magazine, the only periodical published by the Shakers. This position he still holds. The magazine is well gotten up, and contains much interesting matter, not only to Shakers, but to the world's people.

The Shakers very early saw the advantages which would accrue from labor-saving devices, and their workshops, laundries, dairies and kitchen departments are fitted with the very best and latest improvements for making labor easy. The kitchen of the Church family at Canterbury would gladden the heart of any housewife in the land. In the cooking department—in fact, in every department of female labor, the Sisters take their turns in doing the work each month, so that continuous labor in any one department does not fall to the lot of any Sister. For instance, the bakery is in the charge of two Sisters, who arise at five o'clock in the morning and have their work finished by noon. They bake the bread, pies, cake, and whatever else may belong to the bakery. Those who take charge of the general cooking for the family are in another part of the house, and may do all the baking that comes under their charge. At the end of the month they resign their charge to two other Sisters, and pass into another department, thus giving all the Sisters an opportunity to become expert in every department of female labor.

In every room where a fire is needed, a wood-box, built into the wall, with a trap door near the stove, so that no wood or dirt is to be seen, is a feature characteristic of the Shakers. In the large family dining-room, ample for seating sixty persons, is a long table, with the vinegar cruets suspended over the table, and low-backed chairs—low enough to stand clear under the table when not in use.

SHAKER VILLAGE, ENFIELD, CONN.

Lucy Ann Shepard.

The same air of neatness that pervades the laundry is found in the dairy. The cows are milked by the men at six o'clock in the morning, driven to the pastures by the boys, and are driven back to the stables and milked again at five in the afternoon. There is no yelling, scolding, whipping nor maltreating of either cattle or horses; and no dog runs barking, snapping and biting at the heels of the cows—no dog ever finds a home in a Shaker Community.

A visit to the school room at the Shakers is full of interest. Here the children, who have been placed with the Shakers to be reared until they have reached their majority, are educated. And here, it may be truthfully said, they receive the very best common school education. Students graduating from a Shaker school are well fitted to battle with life in any capacity in which they may be placed. The young girls are taught music and have certain hours in the lecture room every day which are devoted to music, reading, talking and visiting.

The Shakers are firm believers in the "early to bed, early to rise" maxim, therefore, as the clock strikes nine, all retire to their couches, to arise with the morning sun.

The dress of the men is plain but neat, like that of prosperous farmers. Formerly they made their own cloth and dressed all alike in uniform color, but now they find it more economical to purchase the usual grade of suitings more in conformity with the world's people. The women still cling to the style of garments adopted in the infancy of the institution, and may be seen in their little lace caps, uniform in style, generally a dress of gray material, and the well-known Shaker bonnet. They are often seen in Concord, N. H., on shopping excursions, in the company of some Elder or Trustee as an escort.

Standing conspicuous among the saintly characters in the Shaker Community was the person of Mary Whitcher, so long and so favorably known to all who ever visited the Shakers at their beautiful home at Canterbury. She might well have been called the Shaker poetess, for the Shaker literature was often enriched by her poetical pen. Mary Whitcher was born in the town of Laurens, Otsego County, N. Y., on the 31st of March, 1815, the youngest of four children. When Mary was eleven years of age, her father moved with his family to Shaker Village, Canterbury, N. H. The site of this Society was the old homestead of Mary's grandfather, Benjamin Whitcher, who, with his wife and children, embraced the Shaker faith, and dedicated their estate to the perpetual use of the Society. There is still standing one ancient apple tree, left to mark that once fruitful orchard of the Whitcher family, and it still yields its annual quantum of fruit.

The Shakers of Canterbury have contributed the following as showing the esteem in which she was held by them: "The youthful Mary being very intelligent and an apt scholar, was early employed as a school teacher, and subsequently appointed to a responsible position with the Trustees, where for twenty years she identified herself with the interest of the Society in a public manner, and became widely known as an ideal Shakeress. Her benevolent nature, ruled by an enlightened conscience, well fitted her to exemplify that immortal utterance of our Savior: 'Inasmuch as ye have done it to the least of these, ye have done it unto me.' None were,too poor or too unworthy to receive her recognition and care. Later in life, she became an active leader in the 'Ministry,' which is composed of two members of each sex, and presides over the two Societies of Canterbury and Enfield, and is the highest office in the Society. This position she retained until failing health compelled her resignation. As her benevolence could not be limited by age or sickness, her good ministries in behalf of her people continued in various ways, particularly in the gifted use of her pen, until her demise, which occurred January 6, 1890, after a patient endurance for six years of intense suffering. The accompanying likeness of her reveals the moral excellence of her character more clearly than any words can describe." The universal verdict, where she was best known, is: "Our Sister Mary was a most lovable, genial, devoted Christian Shaker." It was her pen that wrote:

"Who hath a God, hath all the world beside
In which to live and move and to abide;
But he who trusteth not to power divine,
Doth well distrust beyond the scenes of time."

CHAPTER XVI.

CANTERBURY COMMUNITY—VISIT IN 1854—ATTENDING CHURCH— TABLE MONITOR.

IT was in the month of August, 1854, when I invited a young lady, now the wife of a prominent physician in one of our Western cities, to attend a Shaker meeting on the following Sabbath morning. The invitation was readily accepted by the lady as a novelty she had long desired to witness. It was a beautiful morning and the carriage ride of ten miles to the Shaker village in Canterbury, N. H., was delightful. On arriving at the Trustees' Office of the Church family, we were greeted cordially by the presiding Elder, who, upon learning our mission, extended to us the hospitalities of the Shaker Community.

At the time of our visit, the general public were not admitted to their religious meetings, owing to a tendency on the part of some who attended the meetings to treat the spirit manifestation of the Shaker worshipers with levi-

TRUSTEE'S OFFICE.—UNION VILLAGE, O.

ty. As the time arrived for the hour of service, it was announced by the tolling of the church bell, and we were soon wending our way to the chapel. At the door of the sanctuary the young lady and myself were informed that we must separate, as Shakerism forbade the mingling of the sexes even in divine service. Therefore, as we entered the room, my companion was directed to a seat near the Sisters, while I was conducted to a seat on the other side of the house allotted to the Brothers. Almost the first thing I noticed was a line of black pegs equidistant from each other, and about one foot apart, made even with the floor, to assist the front rank in forming a straight line. As the Brethren entered the room, they removed their hats and coats and hung them upon wooden pegs which lined the sides of the room. The Sisters also removed their bonnets. Then, standing for a moment in perfect silence, they seated themselves, the Brothers and Sisters facing each other. The adults and children were dressed nearly alike. The Brothers in their Sunday costume of blue and white striped pantaloons, with a vest of deeper blue, exposing a full bosomed shirt, with a deep, turned-down collar, fastened with three buttons. The Sisters, in their pure white dresses, with neck and shoulders covered with snow white kerchiefs, their heads crowned with a white lace cap, while over the left arm some hung a white pocket handkerchief. Their feet ensconced in high-heeled, pointed-toed cloth shoes, of a brilliant ultramarine blue. Their faces were full of devout holiness, which marked the occasion as one not soon to be forgotten. For the space of a few minutes the assemblage of worshipers remained in profound silence. Then they arose as by common consent and stood in silence while the benches in the center of the room were removed. The Brethren faced the Sisters, who modestly cast their eyes to the floor, while one of the Elders from the center of the group addressed them with a few words of exhortation. At the conclusion of his remarks, they bowed their heads for a few moments, when they commenced the singing of a hymn:

"God's love is at the helm! We shall outride the storm;
Whose life is in the light can fear no earthly harm.
The passage may be long ere truth o'er error rise;
But they are always strong who make no compromise.

"And since we know the strength of light and love in God,
Shall we be found at length, as those who doubt his word?
Nay, truth our path shall fill, and bring a cloudless sky;
We'll trust and do his will, thus all our foes defy."

This hymn, of which there were several verses, was sung to an appropriate tune, without the use of instrumental music, they all the while keeping time with their feet and with a rocking movement of the body. Then, after a short interval, one of the Sisters in the front rank started the words of a hymn, in which they all joined, marching backward and forward. Their arms were extended at a right angle from their bodies, the palms of their hands turned upward, with a drawing-in movement as they moved on in their march.

At the close of the hymn, the Elder in charge of the meeting, came forward as the worshipers retired to their seats, and made an address, in which he set forth the superiority of the Shaker life over that of all other denominations, and the impossibility of true happiness in this life, or the life to come, unless the Christ life of virgin purity was lived in our sojourn on earth.

The address was terminated in fifteen or twenty minutes, when another lively tune was started and they began a march in a circle around the center of the room, the Brethren two abreast, leading the column, the Sisters following after in sections of three abreast. In this march as in the former exercise, there was a waving movement of the hands by drawing inward, as if gathering in spiritual good and storing it up for the necessities of the week. Occasionally there was a clapping of hands in perfect concert, this being repeated for several times in succession. In the marching and counter-marching, the worshipers frequently changed their positions, the Brothers reducing their ranks to two abreast, while the Sisters increased their ranks to three, and while in this position the singers stood in the center, the others encircling them twice in their marching. Then, again, they formed themselves in single file and marched around the central body, ultimately forming into four circles, with the singers as a common center. This was afterwards explained as symbolical of the four great "dispensations" as expounded in Shakerism. The first, from Adam to Abraham; the second, from Abraham to Jesus; the third, from Jesus to Mother Ann; and the fourth, the "millennial," which the Shakers claim they are now enjoying as the triumphs of their religion.

The hymns sung were somewhat after the Methodist style, the first verse of one of which read :—

> "Away I have turned from this world's transient glory,
> From evil, and all that the wicked can boast;
> And have set out for Zion. O! hear the glad story!
> To gain, more than gain, what in Eden was lost."

At the close of the singing, one of the Sisters began to rock her body to and fro; at first gently, then in a more violent manner, until two of the Sisters, one on each side, supported her, else she would have fallen to the floor. She appeared to be wholly unconscious of her surroundings, and to be moved by an invisible power. This, then, was a physical manifestation of divine power, such as is now seldom met with in the public meetings of the Shakers. The shaking of the subject continued to increase in violence, and it was with great difficulty that she could be restrained from throwing herself forcibly to the floor. Her limbs became rigid, her face took on an ashen hue, her lips moved, and she began to speak in a clear and distinct voice, every word of which penetrated every part of the room, which was as still as death. Every eye was on the recipient of the gift, every ear open to catch each word as it

fell from her lips. She spoke of the shortness of life, of the absolute necessity of abandoning the world and its sinful pleasures before it was too late;
that in Shakerism was embodied all the virtues. and none of the vices, of
mankind; that through her the spirit of Mother Ann was speaking to every
Shaker present to remain steadfast in the faith, and they would enjoy the
richest of heaven's blessings—an eternity of bliss. For the space of fifteen
minutes she spoke rapidly, yet impressively, her whole frame shaking from
head to foot. Gradually the "spell" left her, and her limbs relaxed as she
sank into a seat completely exhausted.

This event clos d the exercises of the meeting. and all left the place pro-
foundly impressed by the solemnity of the occasion. One thing was very
noticeable, the entire absence of prayer during the exercises. Was it possible that the Shakers did not believe in the efficacy of prayer? Was it not passing strange that nowhere in any of their writings was this feature, so prominent in all other Christian denominations, made mention of as any part of
their religious duty? This was afterwards explained to me that the Shakers
generally made their prayers in silence and not in public assemblies.

Those who have visited the Shakers in the past, and have been entertained
by them in the public dining hall, will recall one feature of the table which
was in vogue thirty-five years ago as a peculiarity of, at least, the Canterbury
Shakers, if of no other Shaker Community. On being seated at the table, a
printed sheet was handed to the guest, which at first might be mistaken for a
bill of fare, but upon inspection proved to be an injunction to take upon the
plate only what was to be eaten. This little sheet, entitled "Table Monitor,"
was written by a Shaker Sister, Hannah Bronson, a native of Vermont, who
entered the Community about the year 1800. It is full of homely yet perti-
nent truth, and well worthy of reproduction here:

TABLE MONITOR.

"Gather up the fragments that remain, that nothing be lost."—CHRIST.

Here, then, is the pattern which Jesus has set,
And his good example we can not forget;
With thanks for his blessings, his word we'll obey,
But on this occasion we've somewhat to say.

We wish to speak plainly and use no deceit;
We like to see fragments left wholesome and neat;
To customs and fashions we make no pretence,
Yet think we can tell what belongs to good sense.

What we deem good order we're willing to state,
Eat hearty and decent, and clear out our plate;
Be thankful to heaven for what we receive,
And not make a mixture or compound to leave.

We find of those bounties which heaven does give,
That some live to eat, and that some eat to live;
That some think of nothing but pleasing the taste,
And care very little how much they do waste.

Though heaven has blessed us with plenty of food:
Bread, butter and honey and all that is good;
We loathe to see mixtures where gentle folks dine,
Which scarcely look fit for the poultry or swine.

We often find left on the same China dish,
Meat, apple sauce, pickle, brown bread and minced fish:
Another's replenished with butter and cheese,
With pie, cake and toast, perhaps, added to these.

Now if any virtue in this can be shown,
By peasant, by lawyer, or king on the throne;
We freely will forfeit whatever we've said,
And call it a virtue to waste meat and bread.

Let none be offended at what we here say,
We candidly ask you, is that the best way?
If not, lay such customs and fashions aside,
And this monitor take, henceforth, for your guide.

Many of the present generation have doubtless heard the expression "shaker your plate," who will now understand from whence its origin.

CHAPTER XVII.

CANTERBURY COMMUNITY—VISIT IN 1892—PRINTING OFFICE—MUSEUM—SINGING—STYLE OF DRESS—MUSICAL INSTRUMENTS.

BEING recently at my old home in New Hampshire for a few days' rest, I was strongly impressed with the desire once more to cross the threshold of the Shaker Community at East Canterbury, and see for myself how far the rumors which had reached me, that the Shakers were diminishing, were true. Said one of my old friends: "The Shakers are nearly defunct; there is hardly a baker's dozen of them left in Canterbury." Said another: "They are poor, and are selling off all their land in order to make both ends meet. Why, you remember twenty-five or thirty years ago they were manufacturing and selling large quantities of brooms, pails and tubs, and David Parker did a flourishing business in his patent washing machines and the Shaker garden seeds they raised and sold would nearly supply the whole country. There is nothing of this kind carried on there now. I tell you Shakerism has seen its day. They are as dead as Chelsea up there."

To be "as dead as Chelsea," means a good deal in New Hampshire, and I thought if they were really as dead as this, I would like to walk into the graveyard and see if there were any headstones marking the graves of this once flourishing Community. A party of ten was soon made up, and we started from Concord with two double carriages, while a gentleman and his wife from Boston followed in a single carriage. We left the city about ten o'clock in the morning of a beautiful day, just such a day as we often see in the latter part of August in New Hampshire. We took the same old road over which I drove thirty-eight years before on that August Sabbath morning to visit a Shaker meeting. How the memories of the past clouded my vision as we passed house after house and farm after farm, the occupants of which, I was informed, had all passed on. In some instances their sons were harvesting the crops their fathers were wont to gather. In others, the lands had passed completely into the possession of strangers, and I felt like a stranger in a strange land.

After a ride of some two hours, we began to climb the last hill which brought into view a part of the Shaker village. All along each side of the road lay the lands of the Shakers, or, at least, the lands they were once possessed of before they became "as dead as Chelsea." But there was a certain freshness about the land; the ground looked rich, the grass green, bearing such unquestionable evidence of life and activity that I began to doubt the stories of the dead Shaker Community. As we approached still nearer, and the buildings came more plainly to view, I saw that they had just that same feature of neatness about them, and the paint looked just as fresh as it did thirty-eight years before, and as if but recently painted. Certainly, every thing here had the appearance of thrift and prosperity, even if the Shakers were actually defunct.

We drove up to the door of the Trustees' building, where our party alighted and entered the reception rooms, our horses being cared for at the stable. Almost immediately we were waited upon by several Shaker Sisters, one of whom, on learning our wants, left to superintend the preparing of dinner, while two others opened the "store" that they might exchange some of their handicraft for our money, much to the delight of the ladies of our party, who were very glad to bear away with them some mementos of their visit.

After a most substantial dinner (at which we were not even asked to "shaker our plates," the "Table Monitor" of years ago having disappeared, retired, perhaps, to some cosy nook in Elder Blinn's museum as a relic of the table customs of ancient Shaker days,) we were invited by Elder Blinn and Eldress Dorothy Ann Durgin to take a stroll about the grounds and buildings of the Community. This invitation we gladly accepted. Piloted by this most worthy Brother and Sister, who stand as high officially in Shakerism as honors can be bestowed in their Community, we felt highly favored, and more so on account of the apparent willingness on their part, depicted in their frank, open countenances, to fully satisfy our curiosity regarding modern Shakerism.

In the course of conversation, we learned that no change had been made in the doctrines of the church; that the Shakers were as well grounded to-day in the gospel as preached by Mother Ann as were her immediate followers. True, the spiritualistic manifestations were not made as apparent now as a quarter of a century ago, but this of itself had no significance whatever, as waves of spiritualism had often before passed over the Community, lasting for a period of time, then disappearing, to be revived again as the spirit of revelation and inspiration took possession of some worthy Brother or Sister, and through them the path of duty was made more plain, and greater life and zeal given to their religious service.

A notable instance of this occurred in 1827, when they were visited with a spiritual wave which lasted for several years, and then passed on, to be revived again in 1837. This was a still more notable manifestation of spiritualism, from the fact that it first made its appearance among the children in the Community at Watervliet, N. Y., while they were engaged in religious devotion. On this occasion, some of the children passed into a trance state, apparently becoming wholly unconscious of their surroundings. In this condition they seemed to be controlled by an invisible power which took them spiritually from place to place, asking and answering questions through the mediums, or "instruments," as they were designated by the Shakers.

This manifestation soon spread among the adults, who were, on some occasions, thrown into distressing contortions of the body, bowing and twisting themselves in every conceivable shape. Then for a long time they would spin and whirl with great rapidity, at last falling motionless on the floor. Others went into a state of trance and revealed to the congregation the condition of the spirit world, bringing messages from the spirits of departed Shaker Brothers and Sisters to the assembled congregation of Believers. Quite often several of the "instruments" would be in the entranced state at the same time, and with closed eyes would pass and repass each other in entirely new and intricate marches with the utmost precision, all the while singing new and spiritually-improvised songs and anthems, complicated by motions of the hands and feet and a movement of the body, all in perfect time with the spirit of the song.

These visionists not only gave a full and elaborate description of the state of those who had entered the spirit world faithful in the cause of Christ, but with fear and horror they depicted the unhappy condition of those who had passed the portal recreant to the faith, many of the spirits making these "instruments" the mediums through which they uttered solemn warnings to the unfaithful. These manifestations continued in a greater or less degree up to the year 1856, when they gradually faded away. As we passed on through the Printing Office of the Society, we saw several of the Sisters with busy fingers setting type for the September issue of Elder Blinn's Monthly, *The Manifesto*, while the presses were running off the forms which had been made ready.

Passing into the museum department of the Editor's den, in which Elder

Blinn justly takes much pride, we were treated to an exhibition of the manner in which our forefathers, with flint and steel, struck the spark which kindled the flame of the old pine knot, by the light of which they obtained what knowledge they possessed from books, the hours of daylight being wholly devoted to manual labor. Standing by the side of the old eight-day clock, which was noted for having the bearings of its wheels made of ivory, was a closed upright case about the size and shape of the clock. Stepping up to this, Elder Blinn remarked that as a matter of fact every family of the world's people had their skeleton, and with the further remark, "We also have ours," he opened the door of the closet, displaying a full-sized skeleton suspended by a cord. It is just possible that right here we had the solution of the origin of the rumor that the Shakers were fast becoming defunct. Certainly, until now, there had been no visible appearance of it.

The Shaker Sisters have quite an interesting collection of ancient pieces of crockery, some of which were in use one hundred years or more ago. Elder Blinn also has several pairs of the old-style, high-heeled, pointed-toe shoes in his museum, which were worn by the Sisters who were early in the Shaker faith.

We were shown into many of the departments of which I gave a description in a former chapter. In all of them we found the same features of neatness that were characteristic of the Shakers twenty-five years ago, showing plainly that the children of this generation came up just as good housewives as their elder Sisters.

The Shakers in Canterbury do quite a large business in the line of manufacturing the celebrated Shaker-knit underwear, and, until recently, one firm in New York has controlled the sale of all the garments manufactured by them. They have lately added some knitting machines of the newest and most improved pattern, capable of largely increasing their product in this direction.

In the chapel of the church we found assembled a company of Shaker Sisters for the express purpose of treating us to some vocal and instrumental music. They were led by a Brother. The quality of the singing would compare favorably with that in many of our city churches, showing that much careful attention has been given to the subject. One of the hymns sung with much pathos, the words of which impressed me with the feeling that the Shakers were firm believers in the efficacy of prayer.

> "O! Father, to Thy throne we come, in attitude of prayer.
> Our hearts petitioning Thy grace, Thy guidance, love and care.
> We ask for power to control the elements of earth;
> For wisdom to expand the soul unto the higher birth.

"O! bless us with a fervent zeal, to know and do Thy will;
With more abundant righteousness our understandings fill.
That we may walk with purpose fixed, the pathway of the pure,
Fulfilling all the law of grace, Thy favor to insure."

I afterwards learned from Elder Blinn that the Shakers have been, and are, a prayerful, Christian people; but they accept as their guide the admonition of Jesus: "Do not sound a trumpet before thee . . . When thou prayest, thou shalt not be as the hypocrites are: for they love to pray standing in the synagogues and in the corners of the streets, that they may be seen of men." For this, and the further reasons as set forth in the sixth chapter of St. Matthew, in the sixth, seventh and eighth verses, their prayers are made in secret; they do not pray audibly in any of their public meetings.

It was in the chapel that my attention was first called to the change in the color of the dress worn by the Sisters of the Community. They do not all now confine themselves to the same style of dress goods as formerly, but are wearing dresses made from different material and color. Their dresses are made plain, full in the skirt, with plain waists; shoulder capes, one reaching to the waist back and front, and a little over the shoulders at the sides, the other of about half that length; this, with white linen cuffs and a plain white standing collar, crowning all with a white cap made of plain net lace, constitutes now the costume of the Shaker Sisters. And, thus attired, they looked remarkably pretty.

From the chapel we passed into the school-room, which had just re-convened after a vacation of several weeks. The scholars were all girls, as during the summer months the boys are engaged in work about the farm. The day was nearly spent, so that we had the opportunity of hearing them recite only two lessons, one in demonstrating some problems in arithmetic on the blackboard, the other in geography. The scholars certainly showed a proficiency in mathematics and geography which did great credit to their teacher. The exercises closed with the familiar geography song set to the tune of "The King of the Cannibal Islands."

One thing struck me as an innovation. Twenty-five years ago, such a thing as an organ or a piano in a Shaker Community was never dreamed of, but now, scattered over the premises we noticed no less than half a dozen pianos and as many more organs. Upon my expressing some surprise at this, Eldress Dorothy remarked that they felt that something more must be done for the children than formerly, and that this was something they all could fully enjoy.

We noticed several improvements in progress. A new foundation was being built for an enlargement of the kitchen; also, painters were at work painting the outside of some of the buildings.

We were shown a large map of the property belonging to the Shakers in Canterbury, which was from a survey made several years ago at considerable expense. Six weeks were occupied in the survey. Until this was made, the Shakers had always regarded their landed property as consisting of about three thousand acres, but the survey showed the acreage to amount to rather more than four thousand acres. Of this amount, they have sold, but very recently, two lots amounting to about one hundred and sixty acres in all. This did not look like "selling off all their land," or that they were running out very rapidly.

The actual facts in relation to them are these : There are about one hundred and fifty members comprising the Community in Canterbury. The women outnumber the men considerably, and quite a few of both sexes, being advanced in life, it is not expected, or desired, by the Community, that they should take the brunt of the hard work. During the summer months they employ quite a number of hired men to plant the seed and gather the harvest. Of course, this could be avoided if the Society was sufficiently reinforced by young men. There is not a doubt but that they stand greatly in want of new and younger converts. These may be forthcoming before another decade passes. The Shakers are certainly looking forward to it in the full belief that the times are auspicious, and ere long will result in large numbers making application for admission to their Community.

In a *resume* of the subject of Shakerism, and in arriving at the correct solution as to its remarkable success as a communal body, outlasting by many decades that of all its congeners, we find nothing obscure or metaphysical about it. It is a society of individuals who fully believe in a life of virgin purity as taught and lived by Jesus. It is composed of those who collectively and individually have made it a duty of their daily life to take home to themselves the injunction, "take my yoke upon you and learn of me, for I am meek and lowly of heart." "Abhor that which is evil; cleave to that which is good." "Do unto others as ye would that they should do unto you." This, with the firm belief that Jesus and his disciples, had all things in common, so they must have one purse, one mind, and one purpose, in order to fully enjoy the millennium—the thousand years reign of Christ on earth—which Shakerism teaches, is now being enjoyed by all true Shakers.

That the Shaker Communities are not as flourishing in point of numbers as once they were, is not to be wondered at when it is taken into consideration that their population is not increased except by the voluntary admission of persons who are willing to put off the world and all its worldly pleasures, and take up the cross of self-denial that they may live lives of absolute purity.

The Shakers hold that they see in the "signs of the times"—in the great strife between capital and labor—a tendency towards communism that will result in large accessions to their ranks at no very distant day, as the principles of their religion become better understood by the masses.

CHAPTER XVIII.

ELDER F. W. EVANS—HIS BIRTH—LIFE AT CHÀDWICK HALL—
EMIGRATION TO AMERICA.

ON Tuesday morning, the 7th of March, in this present year, one of the largest and most influential of all the New York dailies made this announcement in their obituary column :

"Elder Frederick William Evans, one of the oldest Shakers in the United States, died in Lebanon, N. Y., yesterday, in his eighty-fifth year.   He had long ago retired from active service as Trustee and from the Ministry, in both of which capacities he had done great good for the Society, not alone in Lebanon, but all over the world.   He was a student, lecturer, author, thinker, and a practical Christian, a man of knowledge, ability, and experience, and one who will be greatly missed."

We might pause here with profit for it is hardly possible to pay a more brilliant and deserving tribute to the memory of Elder Evans than these brief lines convey.   Still, as there are incidents of great interest in the early life and subsequent career of this noted Shaker, who, for sixty-three years, resided with the North Family of Shakers at Mount Lebanon, where for fifty-seven years, and until last November, he was a presiding Elder, we are constrained to devote a few pages to the history of this remarkable man.

Elder Frederick William Evans was born in Leominster, Worcestershire county, England, on the 9th of June, 1808.   He came from a race of long lived yeomanry, his grandfather having nearly reached his one-hundredth birthday at the time of his death, while his grandmother lived to the ripe old age of one-hundred and four years.   His father, George Evans, who was the youngest of twelve children, failed to enjoy the remarkable vigor of his parents and died in early manhood.   When a young man he entered the English army, where he served under Sir Ralph Abercrombie in the Egyptian expedition, co-operating with the fleet under Admiral Nelson on the Nile, where he held a commission.

The mother of Elder Evans, Sarah White, was from a more aristocratic lineage, and her marriage with George Evans was contracted against the wishes of her parents, and was the cause of much unpleasantness between the two families, which resulted in an estrangement that was not removed until her death, which occurred when Frederick was but four years of age, and then only were they so far reconciled as to offer her little son a home in their residence at Chadwick Hall, rear Leaky Hill, the scene of one of Cromwell's battles.

ELDER FREDERICK W. EVANS.

For the account of his life at Chadwick Hall we are largely indebted to his "Autobiography of a Shaker," written by request and published in the April and May issues of the Atlantic Monthly, for the year 1869, and which was republished in 1888, in Glasgow, Scotland, incorporated with some other Shaker articles which were issued from the press bearing the same title.

His life, until he had reached the age of eight years, was much like that of other children of his station in society, except, perhaps, that he was left more to himself, to romp and play with such of the servants as he saw fit to choose as his companions, no attempt being made to interest him in books, of which he knew absolutely nothing, and for which he manifested a great dislike. But it was now decided that he should be sent to school. Thereupon he was placed in an institution of learning at Stourbridge, where there were some two hundred scholars, and where he immediately took rank as "the poorest scholar in school." His stolid indifference to his books and incorrigibility soon terminated his connection with the school, of which he says: "If there was one thing more than another that I hated it was school books and an English school-master, with his flogging proclivities."

On leaving school he again took up his old home life at Chadwick Hall, his mother's relatives giving up all attempt to further educate and fit him for their station in society. Thus left to himself he was banished almost entirely from the influence of the home circle of his uncles and aunts. There was, however, one person who had not given him up as wholly lost. His grandmother still had faith, that notwithstanding his hatred of books, he would yet make his mark in the world, and so she patiently looked carefully after his religious training, requiring him to say his prayers each night and morning, taught him to read the collect on the Sabbath, directing that the servants accompany him to the services held in the National Episcopal Church, where he was enjoined to remember the text, and where he tells us that he "patiently endured an occasional gentle (?) knock on the head from the sexton's long wand," and, "for all of which," he had "a proper respect." On another occasion, when but a child, he heard for the first time in the church the deep-toned notes of the organ, and cried out in great terror, much to the amazement and amusement of the large congregation present.

If, in his knowledge of books he was most sadly deficient, there was, at Chadwick Hall, a most systematic arrangement of all things which was being constantly brought to his notice. It was an extensive estate where the proprietor was given much to the sporting tendencies customary among the English gentry. The kennels contained a goodly number of the various breeds of dogs, which were kept each in its own allotted apartments. There was "the watch-dog in his kennel, the water-spaniel, the terrier of rat-catching propensities, the greyhound, the pointer and the bulldog," diversified by the "horses for the farm, the road, the saddle and the hunting horse."

There was a flock of five hundred sheep, under the care of a shepherd whose duty was to have them constantly under his watchful eye, changing them from pasture to pasture in the summer months, and folding them in the turnip fields during the winter.

Every field on the farm was tilled systematically, with a rotation of crops, in order that a larger profit and better results would ensue. The land was much like our own New England soil, hilly, with patches of wood and timber. A fine stream of water coursed through the estate, forming on its way five beautiful ponds, abounding in fish, while the woods were well filled with game and a large variety of singing birds. "Here," he says, "I was allowed to educate myself to my heart's content, reading and studying the vegetables and fruits, of which there was a great abundance, and in all of which I was deeply interested." Long years after, when he had become a power among the Shakers, he was asked from what Alma Mater he graduated, when he made this reply:

"My school house was the universe, my maps the landscape of hills and valleys, my books the trees and plants, my teachers the servants and their masters and mistresses; graduating therefrom, I emigrated to America, where I taught myself to read books, and began the study of history. I learned how to think, observe and reason upon theology and the social and governmental organizations of mankind, until I became a materialist, a socialist, a land reformer, and an infidel to all the popular church and state religions of Christendom."

In his boyhood he was often the companion of his uncle John in his trips to the weekly market fairs to dispose of the vegetables and produce grown upon the farm, developing an aptitude for trade quite beyond his years.

When nearly twelve years of age his father and brother made a visit to Chadwick Hall for the purpose of obtaining the consent of his mother's family to their taking him to America, whither they had decided to emigrate. They did not, at first, make themselves known to the lad, but were ushered into the parlor, where, upon referring to the nature of their business, they were strenuously opposed by the grandmother, uncles and aunts of the youth. In this interview they all became very much excited over the disposal of the boy, but as a last resort, agreed to leave the settlement of the question to the lad himself, who was to be called into the room in presence of them all, without being previously informed for what purpose. As the father and brother were entire strangers to the boy it was naturally supposed, by his mother's family, that he would surely object to his removal.

On the entrance of Frederick his uncle asked him which he would prefer to do, remain with them and make that his home, or go with the two strangers present, his father and brother, to reside in America? His answer came without the least hesitation—"I will go to America with my father and brother." This settled it, and he was soon "fixed off" and on his way to Liverpool.

In his Autobiography the Elder says: "At this time, I only knew so much of America as I had heard the common people sing of in a doggerel rhyme which originated in the days of the American Revolution, at the time recruits were being raised for service in the army :—

> "The sun will burn your nose off,
> And the frosts will freeze your toes off;
> But we must away,
> To fight our friends and relatives
> In North America."

They embarked for New York in the month of May, 1820, on the ship "Favor," which was freighted with salt and iron. Young Frederick passed his twelfth birth-day on the sea. He tells us at this time, "I was hardy and healthy, and fond of work, but barely knew my letters, and detested papers and books."

The voyage across the Atlantic, was one of the most tempestuous, he heard the Captain say, of all the twenty-two he had made. Three times the jib-boom was broken sharp off close to the prow of the ship, and on one occasion, during a severe blow, the vessel sprang aleak and all hands were ordered to man the pumps.

On landing in New York they went up the Hudson to Newburg, where they contracted for three teams to convey their baggage to Binghamton, where two of his father's brothers had previously located.

He speaks of the contrast, intellectually, between himself and his brother George Henry, who was but two years his senior, and says: "George had received a scholastic education, so that in literary knowledge, we were the two extremes of learning and ignorance, but we were brothers in a higher meaning of the term. We were radicals in our idea of civil government, and in religion, Materialists."

CHAPTER XIX.

SCHOOL LIFE—APPRENTICED TO THE HATTER'S TRADE—GEORGE HENRY EVANS—"YOUNG AMERICA"—ITS PRINCIPLES—COMMUNISM—JOINS THE SHAKERS—LITERARY WORK— END OF AN ACTIVE LIFE.

THE superior intellectual intelligence which characterized George Henry Evans, made a deep impression upon his brother Frederick, and determined him to seek for the golden treasures, he now began, for the first time, to realize, was stored up in books. He says :—

"I now took a sudden turn in respect to books and learning. I saw that knowledge was not only power, but it was also respect and consideration. I made up my mind that I would learn to read and love to read. My first dose was the 'Life of Nelson;' then I set myself to reading the Bible through by course, and I did it. And here I made a discovery, or rather my friends did, that my memory was so retentive that whatever I read was, as it were, pictured on my brain. I had only to look at the picture to see it in all of its minutest particulars without any effort."

From Binghamton he was sent to Ithaca and placed under the care of an Episcopal clergyman who proved a most valuable friend. He tells us that, "One of his first lessons was to teach me how to think. He had only a dozen scholars and we were all well attended to. I became with him a great favorite, and the times of intermission were largely devoted to my special instruction and benefit. At parting he advised me 'always so to live that I could respect myself,' and that has ever since been my life motto."

On leaving this school his father bound him out to learn the hatter's trade, with a manufacturer at Sherburne Four Corners, N. Y. Here he had access to a library of valuable books and improved every moment of his spare time in reading such books, he says, as "Rollin's Ancient History, Plutarch's Lives of Great Men, The Tattler, The Spectator, and Zimmerman, Shakespeare, Watts, Young, Thompson, Socrates, and Plato. I also took up Theology and asked myself why I was a Christian and not a Mahomedan, or a follower of Confucius, for I had read the Koran and the Bibles of all the nations that I could obtain. I read Locke 'On the Human Understanding' and 'The Being of a God.' This laid in me the foundation of Materialism. For I came to the conclusion that matter was eternal, had never been created. I read Thomas Paine's 'Crisis' and 'Rights of Man,' together with Volney and Voltaire, and became a settled and confirmed Materialist; a believer in matter, as I then understood it, the object of my external senses; for I did not then know that I had any other senses."

For the next ten years he kept up the most intimate relations with his brother George Henry, who was apprenticed to a firm in Ithaca, and was beginning to make for himself a name as a free thinker, and a champion for the rights of the human race, in his publication, quite some little time before his majority, of "The Man."

George Henry was also the originator of the land movement in America, on the principle laid down by Thomas Jefferson, that "The land belongs to man in usufruct only." He had the support of Horace Greeley, who, at the time of the birth of the New York Tribune, was one of his warmest and fastest friends.

Frederick, on the termination of his apprenticeship, joined his brother George in the publication of "The Workingman's Advocate," "The Daily Sentinel," "The Bible of Reason," "Young America," and many other papers of like tenor.

The character of the principles expounded in "Young America," were plainly set forth in the head lines of that sheet:—

First—"The right of man to the soil: Vote yourself a farm."

Second—"Down with monopolies, especially the United States Bank."

Third—"Freedom of the public lands."

Fourth—"Homesteads made inalienable."

Fifth—"Abolition of all laws for the collection of all debts."

Sixth—"A general bankrupt law."

Seventh—"A lien of the laborer upon his own work for wages."

Eighth—"Abolition of imprisonment for debt."

Ninth—"Equal rights for women in all respects."

Tenth—"Abolition of chattel slavery and of wages slavery."

Eleventh—"Land limitation to one hundred and sixty acres,—no person after the passage of the law to become possessed of land. But on the death of every land monopolist his heirs are each to inherit only his legal number of acres, and be compelled to sell the overplus, using the proceeds as they pleased."

Twelfth—"Mails in the United States to run on the Sabbath."

The majority of the people regarded these measures as highly chimerical; others as inflammatory and seditious. Their advocates were ostracized as instruments of evil, who were sowing vile seeds of discord and discontent. But the enlightened observer will note that nearly every one of these advocated measures are now the laws of the land in almost every State in the Union, thus establishing conclusively the superior intellectual discernment of these young champions of sixty years ago.

A few years later, George and Frederick Evans became deeply interested in the great experimental wave of Communism which was then spreading over the Middle and Western States.

Frederick, anxious to know something of the practical workings of the institution which promised so much for the amelioration of the human race, decided to visit a society which had been recently established under the leadership of a Dr. Underhill, in Massillon, Stark county, Ohio, and walked almost the entire distance to accomplish his purpose. He did not find this Community in such a flourishing condition as he had anticipated. Troubles were brewing. Inharmony was the prevailing feature, and within two short months after his arrival the institution went to pieces. There was no established religious dogma with which they were in accord. It was a curious mixture of individuals of every shade of belief, infidels, materialists, spiritualists, and a few professors of religion, still it was alleged that too much Christianity was the cause of the failure. Too little Christianity would have been nearer the truth.

Out from the smouldering ashes of this defunct institution about one dozen members resolved to form another association which Frederick was in-

clined to join.   But, in the meantime, he decided first to visit his old home
and relatives in England.   To this end he embarked on a raft from the village of Chautauqua, drifting down the Monongahela and Ohio rivers to Cincinnati, thence on a flat-boat, down the Mississippi to New Orleans where he
shipped for New York, and soon after, in 1829, sailed for England.

It was on this visit that he met an aunt, one of his father's sisters, with
whom he had no previous acquaintance.   To her he made mention of a little
incident that had always been stored up in his memory, but upon which none
of his mother's relatives could give him any enlightenment.   He says:—"It
was the first fact of which I have any recollection and may be of some interest to a student in anthropology.   I saw the inside of a coach, and was
handed out of it from a woman's arms into those of some other person.   My
aunt was utterly astonished at this recital, and informed me that my mother
was coming down from London to Birmingham when I was not more than
six months old, that something happened to the horses which frightened the
party badly, and that I was handed out by my mother into the arms of another person, just as I had seen and remembered."

After nearly a year's absence from America, Frederick took ship again for
New York.   Meeting with his brother and the other members, promoters of
the new Community scheme, he was deputized by the association, in the
month of January, 1830, to travel for the purpose of seeking information respecting the best method of establishing a Communistic society on a sure and
permanent foundation, and for a suitable location therefor.

As a nucleus they had in New York city a "Hall of Science," so called,
from which Robert Dale Owen and Fanny Wright expounded upon the
theory of Communism, and sought to make converts to the new faith.

In the course of a few months Frederick was led, in his travels, to visit
the Society of Shakers at Mount Lebanon, New York.   He tells us that he
went there with the feeling that they were "the most ignorant and fanatical
people in existence."

On his arrival at the headquarters of the fraternity and making known his
mission, he was directed to the North Family as the proper place to begin
his investigations.   He says that he was struck with the air of freedom and
candor with which they met his inquiries, but that after remaining with them
for two or three days, he became satisfied that they were but a society of
Infidels—a complex mixture of Rationalists, Spiritualists, and Christians,
and that it was the first time, in his experience, that he had ever met Religionists who were Rationalists, who were ready to impart a reason for the
faith which was in them.

However, later on, he met with Abel Knight, formerly a staid old Quaker
of Philadelphia, who had passed through the transitory state of Quakerism,
Socialism, and Infidelity, and at last had accepted Shakerism as the true
and only faith.   Abel, while residing in the city of "Brotherly Love" had

made his house the "Sheltering Arms" of all the Communists and Infidels. Being a man of more than ordinary intelligence he was well qualified to cope with Frederick on theology and the peculiar tenets of Shakerism. It was from the reasoning of this man, so we are informed by Frederick, more than aught else, which first impressed him of the truth of the Shaker faith, and the prayers of the Shakers which at last broke down the barrier of infidelity which he had walled up to fortify himself against that Christian institution.

During his stay of three months with this people, he says that he was met in his own pathway by spirit manifestations for weeks in succession, which overwhelmingly convinced him of the existence of a spirit world, and converted him to Shakerism. And in this connection he adds:—

"After three months' absence I returned to New York to face for the first time my astounded materialistic friends, to whom a more incomprehensible change could not have happened than my apparent defection from their ranks. As soon as my arrival in the city was known, there was a gathering at my brother's office, the room was well filled; many older than myself, to whom I had looked upon as my superiors in knowledge and experience, were present. At first there was a little disposition shown by a few to be querulous and bantering, while the greater part took it as a serious matter to be righted by solid argument."

"I called the attention of the company and inquired whether any of them wished to give me any information concerning Materialism and its principles. They all said, 'No; you do not need it.' I then inquired if any one present was acquainted with Shakerism, and again the answer was 'No.' Then, gentlemen, I rejoined, it is for you to listen and for me to speak, and I did speak, giving them as simple an account of my experience thus far as I was able. I also had a separate interview with Robert Dale Owen at the Hall of Science. At the close he remarked: 'I will come up to New Lebanon and stay two months and if I find things as they now appear to me, I will become a Shaker.' I still await his arrival."

Evidently it was not Owen's ambition to walk in the "strait and narrow path" of Shakerism. Frederick returned to Mount Lebanon and eventually became the most noted of all the members of the Mount Lebanon Society.

During his career he has lectured frequently in public. He has been a contributor to seventy different publications. In 1859 he published a "Compendium of Principles, Rules, Doctrines and Government of Shakers, with Biographies of Ann Lee and others." In 1869 he published his "Autobiography of a Shaker," and "Tests of Divine Revelation;" in London, in 1871, "Shaker Communism;" and in the same year he delivered a lecture in St. George's Hall on "Religious Communism," in 1873, published the "Second Appearing of Christ," and for three years, 1873–5 he edited and published, with Antoinette Doolittle as his associate, a periodical entitled "The Shaker and Shakeress."

He was foremost in the discussion of the prominent topics of the day; and while he cast no vote at the polls in any political contest, his ready pen was often employed in battles for justice and equality for all mankind in every walk of life.

Some little time since, in reviewing his years of experience as a Shaker, he used these words:—

"I feel satisfied with the goodness of God and his people to me. I have gained a victory over self which causes my peace to flow as a river, and which fills me with sympathy for all seekers after truth and righteousness, whoever and wherever they may be."

Elder Frederick William Evans was a man remarkably well preserved for one of his years. For sixty years he was a vegetarian, in all that term implies; temperate and systematic in all his habits. A man of robust form and benign countenance; his philanthropic labors commanded the admiration of all. At Mount Lebanon, "To the Society of Believers, he was as a watchman on the tower of Zion; one of her main standard bearers and a mouthpiece from which issued words of eternal truth." He was the "grand old man" of Shakerdom, and will be as sadly missed by as many without the fold as those within the pale of this Christian Community.